Confessions of Joan the Tall

Confessions of Joan the Tall

A Memoir

JOAN CUSACK HANDLER

CavanKerry ❖ Press LTD.

CavanKerry Press Ltd.
Fort Lee, New Jersey
www.cavankerrypress.org

Library of Congress Cataloging-in-Publication Data

Handler, Joan Cusack, 1941-
Confessions of Joan the Tall / by Joan Cusack Handler. ~ 1st ed.
p. cm.
ISBN 978-1-933880-33-4 (alk. paper) ~ ISBN 1-933880-33-3 (alk. paper)
1. Handler, Joan Cusack, 1941~Childhood and youth. 2. Handler, Joan Cusack,
1941~Religion. 3. Girls~New York (State)~New York~Biography. 4. Catholic youth~
New York (State)~New York~Biography. 5. Tall people~New York (State)~New York~
Biography. 6. Women authors, American~20th century~Biography.
7. Bronx (New York, N.Y.)~Biography. I. Title.

PS3608.A7A3 2012
811'.6~dc23
[B]

2012009208

Cover artwork by Carlos Andrade
Cover and interior design by Gregory Smith
First Edition 2012, Printed in the United States of America

MEMOIR
CavanKerry◦Press

In keeping with our thematic emphasis for all of our books on *Lives Brought to Life*, CavanKerry Press is proud to announce the addition of Memoir to our publishing program. *Confessions of Joan the Tall* is the inaugural volume on CavanKerry's Memoir List.

CavanKerry Press is grateful for the support it receives from the New Jersey State Council on the Arts.

for the Cusack family:
Dad, Mom, Catherine, Jerry, even Sonny, and me

Confessions of Joan the Tall

Thanksgiving

The biggest parade of the year not counting of course St. Patrick's Day is Thanksgiving and The Band was marching really early so I couldn't go to 9 o'clock Mass. Usually that wouldn't be a problem cause I could go with Dad to 6:10 in the Monastery but this Thanksgiving because of the stupid water main break in City Island, Dad had to work through the night so I had to get there myself. I set my alarm clock for 5:30, ten minutes to dress and a half hour to walk to the Monastery. But my alarm didn't go off so I woke in a panic that I'd missed Mass and completely ruined the day. Jesus counts on me to come see Him at Mass as much as possible so for sure I couldn't disappoint him on a day like Thanksgiving. I have plenty of things to be thankful for so He has every right to expect me to show up at Mass and say Thanks God before I go off having a great time marching in a parade.

Anyway I grabbed my Woolies, my old lady long johns with the little holes in the shapes of flowers and the ribbon tied in a tiny bow on the undershirt and the legs stretching down to just above my knees so I have to be careful not to fall or sit wrong cause one false move and they'll show under my uniform. And the boys'll never stop laughing over that one. But Mom still makes me wear them. I'll catch my Death of Cold if I don't. Not that I care about colds. I kind of like them. You get to stay home in bed reading Archie comics with Mom making you Beef Tea, her own fancy soup you drink from a cup and she learned how to make from my Grandpa in Ireland. Anyway, I dressed fast in my blue plaid skirt and two sweaters, my favorite red one and the heavy wool green one that scratches the back of my neck but keeps my chest warm Mom says and my tush too. Then I grabbed my boots and stumbled through the dark to the kitchen where I opened the fridge a crack and used that light to put them on. The boots were already too small. Everything I have is too small and my feet're ridiculous.

Anyway I pulled my red stocking hat down almost to my eyes, put on my pea coat and headed for the living room careful not to hit my knees on the frame of the Castro as I passed Mom sleeping in the dark. The wind threw itself at me as I opened the latch and stepped out onto the stoop, then I walked the few steps to the corner and stood on the rocks at the edge of Mr. Geasa's yard. Down the hill to my left one streetlight lit the beach. I could see the waves smashing themselves against the bulkhead the way they do during a winter moon tide or in hurricane season, a few feet more and they'd be over the top and flooding the waterfront houses. But I knew the water would quiet down, it's all show in winter scaring up loud and wild and close to the brim then down again. And it was all show this morning too, just lots of wailing wind that kept the hedges and trees dancing jigs around and over me. But that didn't convince me I was safe.

I looked in the other direction down toward Pennyfield Road that leads out of Edgewater and hooks up with the road to the Monastery. You have to pass The Lots to get to that road, that's where the boys play tricks on the girls as we walk to school. Even though it scares me I like it when they include me in the tricks. But there are Rats in those Lots and long streams filled with green scummy water that smells like sweaty socks and the only time I went in there was once with my brother Sonny. We were going home for lunch and were late cause Sister was yelling at him again so we took the short cut through the swamps so Mom wouldn't be mad and asking any questions. He swore this time he wouldn't tease me and he'd stay right with me but of course he didn't he hid in the weeds and started rustling and making those weird farting sounds so of course I was crying and screaming for him when he jumped out in front of me laughing that stupid Gotcha! laugh of his. I hate it when Sonny tricks me. Sometimes I really Hate him no matter how hard I try not to cause Hate for sure isn't a feeling you should be having about your own brother. Maybe it's even a sin but I can't help it with him always trying to scare me and laughing his brains out when I start to cry.

Once he said he even saw Snakes in those swamps and there was no way to get to the Monastery without walking through them except if I took Pennyfield Road and passed the Crazy Lady's house. She lives in this little brown house with tiny peephole windows like you'd see on a ship and lots of weeds in the yard. The house is all the way back off the road so it's hard to watch that she isn't coming for you and I'm always scared to death she'll see me looking, the boys say if she catches you looking you're done for. You can't run by the house either cause then she'll come after you with a <u>Knife</u>! so the only way to handle things I figure is to walk real straight real fast. Sonny and his friends have seen her, she has wild wiry hair that flies out just like a Witch's does and skinny legs and even a long pointy nose.

Once I dreamed that a whole band of Indians were chasing me, a whole tribe aiming spears and slingshots and bows and arrows straight at me and I was running as fast as I could but everyone knows how fast Indians are so I ducked into an alley. I knew any minute they'd find me there and the only way out for me was to run past the Crazy Lady's house but I was so scared I couldn't move I just stayed crouched there in the corner of the alley with my heart pounding so loud and fast I could feel it down to my belly even my legs were shaking and I woke myself up crying and cold and peeing in my bed and teeth all chattering No way I could pass the Crazy Lady's house even for Jesus so maybe the Lots but the rats and the muck and smelly green water the pounding in my chest and waves against the bulkhead wind scalding my nose and I'm Frozen Oh Lord Please Lord I can't move Please save me pee gushing drenching Woolies stockings filling my boots Joan Joan Mom calling Joan What are you doing standing on that corner it's four o'clock in the morning

Dad, Jesus and Me

It's too bad and I was really really sorry to disappoint Poor Jesus but I never did get to Mass on Thanksgiving. I went back to sleep and this time I really did oversleep and when I got up I had to wash my stinky woolies. On Thanksgiving! Then I threw on my uniform and ran to the firehouse to meet the band. Lucky for me they waited.

But I did go to Mass with Daddy this morning. I love going with him to the Monastery, being so close to him, sitting beside him in the car our breath all foggy and steamy like inside us is real warm and cozy like maybe from our mouth all the way down to the bottom of our throat where the belly is. So it doesn't matter one bit how cold the wind is cause it can't hurt us. It feels like there's this little candle lit inside my chest. I think Jesus put it there and it feels like He's telling me He loves me and He's happy I'm coming with Daddy to see Him. And He's keeping me warm, smiling watching me walk from the car beside Daddy, our boots crunching in the snow. No other sound cause the quiet starts when we close the door to the house. Daddy and I saying nothing, our lips moving a little maybe from the praying, each of us having our own private talks with Our Lord getting ready for Him to enter our souls. And our bodies. It's funny but I feel closest to Jesus when Daddy is there and even closest to Dad when

Jesus is there, it's like they're the same or almost the same and I'm part of them. Everything's better when it's the three of us together.

And one of my totally favorite things about the Monastary is the huge heavy door with about a million Saints carved into the wood that's so old it's almost black. Dad says it's Oak, White Oak. That's so cool, wood that's so dark and dirty out-side can be so light and clean inside. And I'm always so happy to see the huge bright sun shining behind the Saints and I love how it creaks real loud in the dark like it hasn't been opened for a really long time, maybe never. So Daddy and I are really lucky going into this very private holy place kind of like The Catacombs. And Daddy told me once that when the Poor Clares who live in the Monastery die, they bury them un-der the Altar. That's really pretty weird and it scares me a little being so close to all those Dead bodies probably all dust and bones and rosary beads right there under the floor but I push it out of my mind cause I figure Dad isn't scared and besides, Daddy and God are always watching out for me.

It's always so great opening the door in the dark and see-ing the light, millions of little candles flickering like they're dancing, or clapping maybe. Sometimes though I catch my-self wondering how much time a candle's worth in Purgatory time, like how many years or days you get off your burning cause someone's nice enough to light a candle. And is it more at six o'clock in the morning say than 11 o'clock and more maybe in the Monastery instead of the regular Church cause everyone's so completely holy there? But I squash that stuff soon as it pops up.

Inside the big door is a really tiny chapel. The huge door makes it look like it's meant for a Real Church, a pretty big one with a Pulpit and an Altar made of Marble with Huge

Gold Curlicue Candlesticks. And you can feel extra close to Jesus there cause the altar's so close. And no huge ceilings and windows and statues and no zillions of pews and people too that make you feel like you're really far away from Jesus and very very small so how can Jesus if He wasn't God and so perfect and great at performing miracles even see you in a million faces in the middle of Church on Sunday morning? But in the Monastery there'll be only a few other regular Catholics there besides me and Dad. It feels kind of scary being so close to the altar and Father and God, almost as close as the Poor Clares are. Of course they're behind a fence, an iron one like a gate so you can't see them even though lots of times I try to like when Father gives them Communion, I'll try to see a face getting up from the altar rail. But I never can and that's too bad but it's the rule, it's none of my business anyway to be trying to see what they look like.

Just Me and Dad

ostly it's just Dad and me going to Mass at the Poor Clares, but sometimes Catherine comes too. I'm pretty crazy about Catherine, she's totally cool and likes boys and plays basketball. She's even Popular. But still Holy. So it's another nice warm family feeling, Dad, Catherine and me and of course Jesus. And I don't know exactly what Catherine's thinking, but I know how happy I am to have a chance to show Daddy how hard I'm trying to be the girl Jesus wants so I figure Catherine must feel that way too. But sometimes I'm extra Lucky and I'm the only one to go with Daddy. And I am pretty crazy about that but that's for sure being selfish and with Jesus too cause when Catherine comes it's one extra Sacrifice for Him.

Eugene Joseph Cusack

I've been thinking a lot about Sonny, what I said about him being mean and me hating him. That's for sure not being the girl Jesus wants. I don't hate Sonny, I could never hate him, he's my brother I love him. So what about a little teasing? Sometimes he's even great. And he's pretty holy too. He's an altar boy and always goes with Dad to the Holy Name Father and Son Mass and Friday Night Devotions. And he's a really great Artist. See when he was in the 5th grade he met Sr. Mary Scholastica, an old nun with a big wart on her chin right at the spot where it turns into your neck and she always has alot of spit around her mouth when she talks. And her Habit's pretty messy, kind of wrinkled with lots of smudges from chalk. I never knew Nuns were allowed to be messy but Sr. Mary Scholastica is and she's not pretty at all and is even old. But she loves Sonny, she doesn't even care that he doesn't do his homework or pay attention in class, she just likes him and thinks he's going to be a great Artist someday. It's true, Sonny can draw anything. One day when she was talking about Mexico in Geography she walked past Sonny's desk and instead of writing down his Mexico notes that she put on the board, he was drawing pictures of little Mexican farm boys. Of course I don't know how she knew they were farm boys but she did. Maybe they were watching the cows, or maybe the goats. Anyway she called for a meeting with Mom and Dad to talk about Sonny drawing during Geography and guess what? She wasn't mad and complaining that this kid is wasting his time, she was saying that she knows this great art school at the Villa Maria which is a rich Catholic school over in the Country Club Section but the tuition isn't too much cause the classes are on Saturday. She really wanted Mom and Dad to take Sonny to the Villa cause he has this God Given Talent she says and who cares about Geography? What's important is that he gets to draw all he wants. That's pretty nice, a Nun thinking Sonny's art is important. Of course Sonny loves her too, she calls him Eugene, not Sonny like everyone else does. Eugene makes him sound Older and Sophisticated, like he should sound being the great Artist he is.

Anyway Mom and Dad went right down to the Villa to sign him up for the classes and then and there he started winning prizes. One was for a statue of a Mexican man who's wheeling a wagon with a planter that has a cactus in it. Mom hung it in the Dining Room. The next first prize was for a painting of a statue of the Infant of Prague, the Baby Jesus and He's wearing long white robes which I figure are probably velvet and a gold crown and He's holding a gold globe in His hand. That's Dad's favorite painting, Mom hung that one in the Dining Room too. Then Sonny started being the regular artist for The Chantalette our school newspaper and drawing crosses or animals or God or any other thing that Sister needs. His drawings are all over the classrooms, all the Sisters have him working for them. The best is when he paints the classroom windows for Christmas, he makes Huge Baby Jesuses with lots of goats and cows all around and of course the Blessed Mother and St. Joseph. And the three kings and shepherds too. Everybody who was there the night Jesus was born. Anyway, Sonny likes St Joseph so much, he even picked Joseph as his Confirmation name, he likes signing his name Eugene Joseph Cusack.

The Flower Lady

ven though we're not all great artists lots of people in the Cusack Family are talented, like Jerry is for singing and Catherine is for basketball. Mom too. It's like Mom has this God Given Talent for Growing, flowers mostly. I think that's why God picked May for her birthday cause somebody born in May should be good at taking care of everything that's waking up. All you can see are flowers and trees with tiny buds that grow til all of a sudden they just burst open so we have zillions of roses in front of the house and geraniums everywhere else. My favorite is the tree Mom planted in the backyard, it was just a tiny baby then and now it's tall and graceful and all pink. In the spring it blooms deep pink flowers that're almost purple. I like to imagine how they get to be such a beautiful color, the pink getting darker and darker til all of a sudden it's purple. They're like tiny bouquets for my dolls. I don't really <u>play</u> with dolls anymore but I still keep them on my bed, most times they're buried under the clothes pile. And Mom can draw too, she used to sit with Sonny for hours drawing Moon Mullins from the comics. That's the amazing thing about Mom, all of a sudden she's great at something. Without even telling you about it before. She'll just sit right down and crochet a vest for you or make a peach upside down cake or take that old accordian out of the closet and start playing some jig that maybe her Dad taught her. Or she'll grow amazingly Huge Hollyhocks in back of the house that're so tall they hit the bedroom windows. Or make a skirt for me or Catherine. Without a pattern. Lots of stuff like that. Or wallpaper the bedrooms or the bathroom. Once she used Dad's big saw and sawed a dresser in half so she could make two little night stands to put beside our beds, Catherine's and mine and you can't even tell unless you pull out the bed and see the side that's messed up.

God Given Talent

Besides being the Best and Holiest Person I know except for Father and the Nuns of course, Daddy's pretty talented too. He has Huge Muscles in his arms like big fat fists and he reads Blueprints about plumbing lines and foundations and attics and crawl spaces and walls that are held up with steel. And what studs are. I think I might even want to be an Architect cause of all the building stuff I learned from Dad. I even wish I could get an Erector Set for Christmas so I can build my own bridges and stuff but I wouldn't tell anyone cause I already asked for a bike and my Magic Skin Doll. And you can't be a pig asking for everything. Besides who ever heard of an Erector Set for a girl? And I'm already having enough trouble feeling like a girl. But Jerry wants one too so I figure maybe he'll let me play a little with his. And Dad plays the harmonica, every night after the Rosary and before bed Dad'll play for us then give us piggyback rides to the toilet and to bed.

Jerry Too

verybody says that Jerry's so great at singing that he's a Young John McCormack, he's a really famous Irish singer everyone knows about, not my friends and the regular people but all the Irish people. His voice could make you cry, that's what they say and so could Jerry's. And Jerry can do a lot of grown up men stuff too. See he loves to sit listening to Dad's stories about the Shipyards. He likes building too just like me. He's going to be an Engineer in the Air Force. Jerry's only 9 and he's already planning to fly airplanes. And he loves to take apart Dad's pocket watch. Dad calls it his Railroad Watch. But Jerry's most favorite thing is the brown radio and for sure he's an Expert at taking it apart and putting it back together. He's so good at fixing stuff that if he takes the radio apart no-body else can put it together again, even Dad. That makes Mom pretty mad when it's getting close to Friday night and Jerry's out playing instead of putting the radio back together cause then we won't be able to listen to our fa-vorite shows. But Jerry always saves the day. The Cusacks just don't have problems with kids not coming home when they're supposed to, we're too scared of Mom. And Jerry loves going to work with Dad on moonlighting jobs, Dad's the Plumber for everyone in Edgewater and Jerry likes to carry the tools and run around helping the men measuring things and mixing cement and finding the screwdriver or the hammer. Dad calls him Little Joe and all the men are crazy about him too, so they'll call him up to sing for them, Danny Boy maybe.

A Really Great Place

Edgewater's great. It's more like a place you go for Vacation instead of for just living. And for sure it isn't like regular places like apartments where millions of people live in one building all on top of each other. Or those houses with the huge lawns and perfect fake looking grass you can't walk on. And the mailboxes are out by the road instead of nailed to the front of the house. And there are no stoops and for sure no beach. People who live in those places have to take a bus or a car to the beach so they certainly can't go night swimming or swimming in the rain or run home to change into their bathing suit in the middle of the day.

See even though Edgewater's in the Bronx, it's surrounded by water. The Long Island Sound. Like an island almost except one side's land. When we first moved there the houses were still just bungalows. That means they didn't have cellars and stoops and coal furnaces and walls that go all the way up to the ceiling. The walls were the kind they have in bathrooms in school where the wall only goes up to cover a normal person's body but not some stupid Too-Tall Body with the head sticking out over the top so everyone can see that it's you in there! So Dad and all the other Dads went to work right away changing bungalows into houses. We all needed furnaces and cellars and stoops and insulation.

Dad's pretty fussy about our house so he wanted all that stuff especially a fancy cellar like they have in richer houses, one you can play in without worrying about Mom getting mad cause you're messing the couch. And there's even a stove where Mom can cook in the summer instead of sweating her brains out upstairs and a table and chairs so we can eat down there and stay nice and cool. And there are no problems with wet bathing suits, we never have to change even if we're dripping wet. And just in case you want to just flop down and take a nice nap all by yourself, we have a black crumbly looking leather couch. We all race to see who'll get to stretch out on it. And it's maybe not so nice to say but our house is the nicest one on the block. Dad told us that if Fifth Avenue downtown in New York kept going all the way straight into the Bronx and then all the way up to the Long Island Sound it would be our block! So you can almost say we live on Fifth Avenue, not really but almost.

And of course The Dads make sure everyone has their chance. They all have lots of muscles in their backs and their arms that shine and pop out and they don't even wear undershirts but that's okay even if I get a little embarrassed. And they laugh a lot and drink beer. We love it when they send the boys to get more beer or the girls to get the sandwiches the Moms're making for lunch. And usually Mr. Schadel or Mr. O'Shea or even Mr. McNamara will call Jerry over to sing Who Threw the Overalls in Mrs. Murphy's Chowder?

Edgewater Park Girls
Fife Drum and Bugle Corps

y most favorite thing about Edgewater besides the Beach is the Edgewater Park Girls Fife Drum and Bugle Corps. It's pretty cool that someone like me can join such a great thing as a Band. You don't even have to be able to play anything, they just have to have a space for you. Catherine and her friends are all members so I couldn't wait til they had room for me. The luckiest of all is Marilyn, the Majorette and Chief Twirler, she's out in front where everyone can see her doing all her fancy twirls and dances. Of course I'd never want to be her cause besides being taller than anyone else in the whole stupid parade, I'd drop the baton and trip and look like the biggest Gawk with everyone falling down laughing at how dumb I look. But not Marilyn, she has the best uniform, the biggest hat and the fanciest boots and a baton that's decorated with gold and tassles and lots of red and blue stones like rubies. And right behind Marilyn are the Twirlers in the little flare skirts and the big hats with pom pom feathers on top and gold tassels on the shoulders and of course the white cowboy boots with gold tassels too. The Twirlers throw the baton in the air and catch it and twirl it under their legs. It would be so great to be one but I know I'll never graduate to twirler cause for sure white twirler cowboy boots don't come in size 11 Quadruple A.

When I first joined the band I played the fife which I wasn't too crazy about but then a space opened in Drums. I started with the base drum which I wasn't crazy about either, it's hard not to feel like a Big Gawk marching with this huge thing hanging over your belly and your chest all the way down to your knees. It killed my legs banging back and forth on my thighs cause my drum was missing the part that makes it stay in one place so I had to be careful balancing the drum and playing it and making sure my feet were marching left, right, left. Lucky for me I moved to regular drums, I'd been practicing drills every night on the wooden door saddle that separates the kitchen from the Dining Room. And we have lots of Parades, besides Thanksgiving there's St. Patrick's Day and Memorial Day and July 4 and of course Labor Day when we march all around Edgewater followed by the Moms and their kids, not our Mom though. The best Parade of all is on the Saturday before Labor Day before all the swimming races start. Labor Day's the biggest weekend in the summer with picnics and music and lots of parties and everyone laughing a lot. I always wish Mom and Dad would come down to watch the races too but they never do. I guess they're shy. Of course if any of us are in any races they'll probably come down to watch, but all the parades pass our house anyway so they can always see us.

A Pretty Great Day

Sunday's a pretty great day for the Cusacks. We all go to 9 o'clock Mass, the whole family in Gorgeous George. The Family That Prays Together Stays Together, Daddy always says. He learned that from Bishop Sheen who always says that at the end of his TV show. And it's true, Sunday's a pretty great day in the Cusack house. It starts right after Mass with bacon and eggs and hard rolls and buns and orange juice and tea, Mass is over so we don't have to be quiet and praying any more. Right after Catherine and I finish the breakfast dishes, we'll peel the potatoes and Mom'll start dinner, usually roast beef with mashed potatoes or leg of lamb. I totally love leg of lamb, crispy and brown and all juicy inside the way Mom makes it with the roasted brown potatoes. With tiny pieces of browned onions on them, hard and crisp outside then soft like mashed inside. And carrots maybe or spinach but not mashed with the potatoes like she makes for us when there's no company. With lots of butter mashed in. The mashed veggies are just for us not for Company like the regular green and white towels and all the different colored ones that don't match anything, you just use them to dry yourself when the green ones are all dirty. Which is usually all the time with so many people taking baths and washing their feet.

If Mom's able to save some money from the food budget

that week and doesn't owe Sister for our tuition and maybe can not answer the door for Mr. Wrenn the insurance man until maybe next week, Sunday Supper's pretty great too cause we get to have cold cuts and salads and Store Bought Dugan's Chocolate Layer Cake with the great icing that you can peel off and eat like it's candy.

My other favorite is Friday nights all of us together sitting around the radio listening to The Shadow and then Wrestling. I don't care so much about Wrestling but Dad and Jerry and Sonny love it so I stay around and Catherine and Mom too cause it's pretty cozy being there, nobody ever wants to get up and go to bed. Mom'll be up and down in and out of the kitchen making the peach upside down cake or the plum and I'll bring in huge glasses of cold milk. That's what's great about Mom always making you great stuff to eat. Even if you don't like something, Mom will make something special for you like making Catherine creamed fish on Fridays when the rest of us're having flounder fried in the pan. Or the creamed onions or cauliflower when the rest of us're having peas. She does the same thing for me with the parsnips.

†
JMJ

Jobs

Besides Mom and Dad everyone has to work in the Cusack house, that means me and Catherine. Sonny and Jerry don't do housework, boys never do. They just walk the dog and sometimes they take the garbage out. And if I'm not around they'll go to Braren's to get milk or peanut butter maybe or to Tony's for potatoes. So me and Catherine do everything else. Catherine does most of the cleaning, the dinner dishes and vacuuming and washing and waxing the kitchen floor and dusting and polishing the Dining Room table and the coffee table and even the piano. She likes to give everything the Catherine Look, that's her name for it. I cook dinner and clean the stove and sometimes the fridge and the bathroom but Catherine never likes the way I clean the tub so she just gets the Ajax out and cleans it again. I <u>scour</u> the pots. I don't even have to, Catherine never does, she just uses the regular dish soap and hot water to clean them but I want them shining. I love it when Dad brings home the Brillo pads from Safeway so I can really make the pots sparkle. It's weird how I really like a sink full of messy pots that I can make shiny and beautiful again.

Favorites

oday's no school but only for the Catholic kids. When I was a little kid I thought there were two religions, Catholic and Public and you could tell right away what religion a kid was if you knew what school they went to. Us Cusack kids went to St. Frances so you knew right away we were Catholic but all my friends except Virginia went to PS which means Public School 72 so you knew they were Public. I used to feel sorry for the Public kids cause they weren't Catholic so part of the One True Religion and I worried that they wouldn't be Saved. I tried not to think about it cause God takes care of everything, but it kept popping up. I didn't understand why God would make us part of the One True Religion and our friends Publics, like He liked us more. That used to make me feel really bad and really scared for them. For sure I didn't want them going to Hell or even Limbo but then I found out God'll save all of us if we're good, even people who aren't lucky enough to be Catholic. That made me really happy about my friends but so awful for not trusting God. If my Faith was strong enough I'd never worry about God Playing Favorites.

St. Joseph Daily Missal

his afternoon's Confession. And for sure, I'm going cause a lot of Bad Thoughts keep jumping up inside my brain specially that stuff about Sonny and God Playing Favorites. They're for sure sins. So I try hard to push them out by thinking and thinking about something that makes me really really Happy like my Birthday coming or my Confirmation or Christmas which it almost is. And all the presents I'll get. And besides what Mom and Dad'll give you which is always totally great, you can't wait to open Catherine's present cause you know you're going to totally completely love it. See Catherine's great at picking the perfect thing to give you which you're maybe dying for. And all of a sudden you feel all warm and soft inside yourself and pretty too cause it's your birthday and your big sister wants you to have this really perfect thing. Catherine taught all of us to do that, to love buying each other presents. Besides Mom and Dad of course always buying us millions of presents for Christmas and even our birthday.

One of my favorite presents from Catherine is my St. Joseph Daily Missal just like Dad has, a big fat black book made of leather I think that has all the prayers the priest says during the Mass. And all the prayers we say and the Altar boys. And the Hymns, all the beautiful songs that the Choir sings or just the regular people. And it has the prayers for Benediction and the Litany of the Blessed Mother, all sorts of stuff you need if you're a Catholic and go to Mass which you for sure do. It's written in Latin and in English with lots of bright colored ribbons that you can use as bookmarks. I really love it and I always get such a nice warm feeling seeing it there on the pew holding my place when I come back from Communion. I can't wait for the day when it's so old that it has the smudges at the top of the page from me turning them so many times like Dad's has. I think it's so cool when people like Dad lick their finger a little and use the wetness to turn the page so the pages get all smudgy from being used so much. And Catherine gave it to me for my Confirmation. Dad gave Catherine hers. For a second just now I almost thought maybe it isn't fair that Dad gave Catherine her Missal and not me too and of course the boys but that's being Selfish and Stingy and totally completely Ungrateful about someone as great and generous as your sister I'm so sorry Dear Jesus to be always thinking about myself instead of being more Charitable and Loving My Neighbor as Myself even though Catherine isn't my neighbor but my sister who probably I'm supposed to love even <u>more</u> than myself. It really <u>is</u> nice that Dad did that for her.

Washing Your Soul

I try to be really really careful with My Soul. I'm not even sure what it is, not like my body that I'm pretty clear about. But the Soul's different, you can't see it and it's more Important than anything. I figure it has to be somewhere inside the body. For a while I thought maybe it filled in the spaces between my heart and my belly, another time I decided it was in my left arm up close to the top where we get our vaccination. And the Soul's round too I think, like a cupcake, the bottom part where the paper is. That sounds kind of weird but it seems like a pretty good answer to the Not Being Able to Picture It and Where on Earth Is It Soul Problems I'm always thinking about. And the color changes, before Confession it's all dark grey and smudgy but after Confession and Penance it's all white and pure. I like thinking of the grey disappearing and my soul being all clean and white again. More than anything I want a Clean and Pure Soul.

Poor Jesus

God's so great, always helping me clean up my soul by suffering and dying for my sins which I for sure don't deserve but He did it anyway cause He loves me so much. Not just me, the whole rest of the World too. Well it wasn't exactly God Himself meaning God The Father who did the suffering and the dying, He sent Jesus who I guess said Okay when The Father asked Him to do it. I always feel so sorry for Jesus. And Guilty too, I mean I'm not sure He really <u>wanted</u> to be Crucified and Die for our sins specially when He called out in the Garden, Father take this cross from Me. We all figure that maybe He didn't want to go through with it and wished He could change His mind. I can imagine how He felt and it's for sure pretty Awful. But I figure God and Jesus must have worked this out between them, they're Father and Son so they're mostly partners. And anyway I'm sure they don't have the kinds of problems us humans have complaining and saying this isn't fair and being really unhappy and maybe scared. That helps me a little in my Worrying and feeling Sorry and for sure pretty Guilty about all that Poor Jesus had to do for me and the rest of the world.

So He for sure deserves sacrifices, every single one that you can think of cause you should always be hurting for Jesus. That's why I love Mass in the Monastery. Those're Special

Sacrifices so they're a good chance to make Jesus happy. And going to Mass when you don't have to specially in the freezing cold at 6 o'clock in the morning lets you feel maybe a little bit more like the girl Jesus wants and for sure He deserves. But you can't let yourself think that too long. Always remember you're just a Sinner, Daddy says and Sister too and Father at Mass and even our Catechism and nothing you can ever do even going to Mass every day at 3 o'clock in the morning maybe in a blizzard can make that not true. No matter how hard you try you'll always disappoint Jesus. And it's not that He says that, He'd never say that, He's always loving you even though you mess up alot. But it's true we're always hurting God so you for sure can't be letting yourself sit back relaxing that you're treating Him right.

Like a Bride Almost

But there's one day when your soul is the cleanest and whitest it's ever been and you're almost sure, not completely but almost that you <u>are</u> the girl that Jesus wants and that's your First Holy Communion Day. It happens when you're in second grade and it's the Best Day of your life and you wish it could last forever. That's the first time you're allowed to Receive, after Father changes the bread and wine into Christ's Body and Blood. After that you can be lucky enough to receive Jesus as many times as you want except only once a day of course and only at Mass, except if you're really old and dying and extremely sick. Then Father can bring it to your house, the Host that's already turned into Jesus's Body and Blood and maybe leftover from this morning's Mass. And when you Receive Father puts the Host on your tongue and then you swallow not chewing cause teeth for sure aren't holy so they should never get near it, the Host I mean. Then it goes into your belly which can't have anything in it either that could touch and mess up the Host. So you have to be Perfectly Clean. Specially your Soul, it has to be Totally Completely White too like a brand new baby's <u>after</u> Baptism. Baptism's the Sacrament that washes away the Original Sin that Adam committed that we all have to get rid of if we want to ever see Jesus in Heaven.

Except for the babies that aren't baptized. Sister says they have to go to Limbo <u>Forever</u> where they just float around maybe in the clouds, kind of like Heaven except Jesus and the Blessed Mother and all the Saints and Angels aren't there. So it's not really happy and bright and beautiful, it's kind of dull and grey colored with no Jesus around. Only the babies are there, which if I had any problems with my Faith I might think wasn't fair cause they didn't do anything so why can't they see Jesus? But whatever Sister and the Catechism say, God says so I just squash the question as soon as it tries to pop up in my brain.

And what's so great about God is that He invented a Sacrament that helps you wash your Soul when it gets dirty. To make sure you don't have even the tiniest little venial. Before you do anything else like have your bath or have Mom put your hair in rags, you have to say Penance, that means you go to Confession and tell the priest all your sins and then say your Our Fathers and Hail Marys and maybe even Apostles Creeds if you have alot of sins to get rid of. And you're all ready to Receive when you've finished your Penance and every single part of your body inside and out so your belly and your throat even and your hair and your ears too and of course your fingernails are totally perfectly clean. With not one spot on them anywhere cause even the tiniest spot or piece of left-over food or dirt would be disrespectful and probably a sin if it touched the Host. And perfectly clean means every bit of clothes you wear too. Everything brand New.

So you think I'm the Luckiest girl in the world Receiving for the first time, an almost Grown Up Catholic walking around with Christ's Body and Blood inside me even though I'm only in second grade. I'm almost as clean and pure as a Saint which of course I know I'm not but this moment I'm the closest and cleanest ever. And I'm really Happy and lucky too cause I get to wear the beautiful white lacey Bride's Dress except short, not long and even the veil but not over my face. And I have sparkly shining new Mary Janes and white socks that have a tiny tiny row of lace on top and a really pretty pocketbook that's more like a little sack with a fat cord type ribbon that I pull to close it. And everything's new, more even than Easter cause every once in a while you have to wear the same coat maybe as last year cause who has money for brand new clothes for every single kid every year? But for your Communion every single thing is <u>for sure</u> new. Even your underpants and barrettes. So you look all Beautiful for Jesus even if you're a little ugly or even just homely which isn't completely ugly but for sure not pretty either.

Sonny and Joan

In the summer when there's no school, I go to Mass at 9 o'clock in the regular Church. Sonny comes too. But those days I kind of mess up the Sacrifice I think cause it's embarrassing to say but it's true so I have to, I love to carry my St. Joseph Missal right out where everyone can see that I have one. That's Showing Off Sonny says. He doesn't like carrying his and he doesn't want people to notice him going to Mass. Not me though, I think you can even say I want everyone to see me with my Missal. I don't even know if Sonny would tell Dad he goes to Mass if I didn't. Not that I exactly tell him but maybe I'll say, You know who I saw at Mass this morning? or something like that. I can sort of hint so you'll find out without me being completely guilty of Bragging which is really Pride. Thinking and saying you're really Great is for sure a sin of Pride and that's not something you'll ever see Dad doing. Not Sonny either. And the sacrifice is no good anymore cause you told somebody, as soon as you talk about it it's ruined.

Anyway Sonny and I are the only ones going to 9 o'clock Mass in the summer, Catherine already has a job at Woolworth's at the Square so she can't go with us and Jerry's still a little too young to be worrying about making Sacrifices for Our Lord. He's not worrying yet about being a Sinner either

†
JMJ

I don't think. But Sonny and I received our Confirmation already so we know how important it is for us to be going to Mass any time we can and for sure the summer's one of those times. I always have such a nice warm feeling inside me walking to Mass with Sonny, he's not teasing me or playing scary tricks on me and that feels so nice. He's really careful about being the right kind of person going to Receive so he doesn't even <u>try</u> to scare me walking down the Fort Road telling me about the Rats and Snakes when we pass the Lots and get to the spot where the Monsters and Snakes can come out at you. And he doesn't make me walk closest to them either which he always does on school days when Mom makes him walk with me, he lets me walk out by the road where I can run really fast if anything like a Monster or a Crazy Dog or a Rat maybe jumps out and comes after me. And I'm not one bit scared, not of him and not of monsters, I'm not afraid of them cause I have my Big Brother with me.

After Mass sometimes we stop in the Italian lady's candy store right across from Church to buy some Double Bubble or Bazooka or Good and Plenty for me or Three Musketeers for him. But we put the candy in our pocket til after we get home and have our glass of water to wash down the Lord. Really the Host. You never know if a tiny piece of Host might have gotten caught in your mouth or your throat so you have to make sure to rinse your mouth after Communion so God's body doesn't get messed up with the candy.

Nocturnal Adoration Society

Sonny gets extra chances to Sacrifice cause he's 13 already so he joined The Nocturnal and goes with Dad. The real name is Nocturnal Adoration Society and it's only men, no ladies. It's Dad's favorite cause it gives you a chance to do something extra special for God. What you do in Nocturnal is you keep the Blessed Sacrament company while it's Exposed on the Altar all night on the First Saturday. Adoration always starts at 9 o'clock after First Friday Devotions and Benediction which is always the last thing that happens at night in Church. The priest shakes the gold pots and the really smelly smoky Frankensense stuff comes out and makes a little trail of white smoke like a lacey cloud maybe or a see through veil. And you and the whole Church will be singing Tantum Ergo and Oh Salutaris and you'll be crying like your heart's breaking just like you do at Mass during Communion when everyone sings Oh Lord I Am Not Worthy cause you're so so happy to be here with Jesus. Nocturnal starts when the singing stops and Benediction's over. All of us regulars go home but the Nocturnal Men like Dad and Sonny have to kneel with the Blessed Sacrament and pray for an hour during the night. And of course you have to be kneeling, an hour of kneeling and praying.

But maybe sometimes you'll have to go at 3 o'clock in the

morning. Or 4. That's the time Dad likes best, he even <u>volunteers</u> to go in the middle of the night so he's <u>sure</u> he'll have the hardest time and so the Biggest Sacrifice. He totally loves the chance to suffer for the Lord so he wouldn't think he was lucky if he got to go at 9. I know inside myself I'd be happy if I got 9 o'clock or even 10 so I could sleep more. Either way I'd be Disappointing Jesus. Sometimes I even think maybe I'm lucky to be a girl so I can't go to Nocturnal cause I know I'd be pretty Scared alone in the pitch black night with only the lights for the Souls flickering and the Monstrance, that's where they keep the Host, on top of the Altar looking all holy holding the Blessed Sacrament but making weird monster shadows on the ceiling. And the Monstrance'll be watching me and looking out at me like a gold sun, the Host which is The Eucharist, the Body and Blood of Our Lord Jesus Christ at the center and all the gold rays coming out from that cause it shines so much. But I'd be getting really scared thinking about staying for a whole hour alone in the dark Church in the middle of the night with only The Host for company. That's when I start feeling ashamed and my stomach starts to burn and a loud mad voice starts yelling <u>How can you be scared? Isn't God Himself right there in the Monstrance? Don't you even believe Him when He says He's always watching over you? Where is your Faith?</u> Faith's the thing that you can't be a Catholic without, it means believing no matter what, even if you can't see it or it doesn't make any sense. Like believing totally and completely that God's there watching out for me 24 hours a day 7 days a week rain or shine. Even if there's a Plague or a War. He still can be here kneeling beside me in the pitch black dark. That's when I start feeling Scared and really really Ashamed for doubting God.

I'll bet Sonny never doubts God. Dad says he gets up every time without a sound. And for sure he never has even one little complaint like I'm tired or it's so dark. Dad's pretty proud of him for that I think and I'm sure Sonny feels real good to be able to show Dad how Happy he is to Sacrifice for Our Lord. I wish I could be Happy to Sacrifice, not just sometimes but Always, for Jesus and for Dad.

Breaking God's Heart

I don't think Daddy <u>ever</u> has Bad Thoughts. He isn't only holy and perfect during Mass or Nocturnal or at night when we say the Rosary or Sacrificing during Lent or Advent, he's <u>always</u> thinking about God and being God's Servant. Nothing's <u>ever</u> more important than that, even us. God always comes first and for sure he's right about that. God deserves every bit of attention we have, every waking second we should be thinking about Him. And for sure Daddy really does that, I never met anyone who's closer to Our Lord Jesus Christ or treats Him better than Dad. I want so much to love the Lord the way he does. We can never do enough for Him Daddy always says, all of us such sinners. But the Lord accepts us anyway even though we'll <u>never</u> be good enough. Dad even says <u>he's</u> just a poor sinner too Disappointing God with his Weakness, always being Tempted by Satan. The way Dad talks it seems like the only ones who come close to loving Jesus as He should be loved are the Blessed Mother and the Martyrs. I don't think even St. Joseph and the regular saints who're just holy but didn't burn at the stake or get eaten by lions or have their heads chopped off love Him enough.

I try so hard to make God Most Important. I pray that someday I can care more about Him than about a single other thing but still I know I don't really <u>always completely</u> love Mass the way I should like Dad does. Sometimes we'll be kneeling for a very long time and I'll be following the prayers not even thinking about my knees hurting or my back and we'll be getting close to Communion and all of a sudden I'll be thinking of sitting back cause it feels so good when you just plop your tush back against the pew but then the hating myself starts and the shame when I think about The Lord and the nails in His palms and I can't even kneel for a minute without complaining like a Big Huge Baby about hurting. And even though the complaining's not out loud, God can still hear it cause He can read my thoughts so He must feel really bad that I can't even kneel through one little Mass. And I can see on Daddy's face that <u>he</u> isn't thinking about his back hurting. And I know for sure he's not wondering what's for breakfast.

Aunt May

unt May's coming tomorrow. She always comes on Saturdays, not every Saturday just once every month. I really love Aunt May. She's Dad's sister and what's so amazing is she's a Nun, except she's really really nice and never yells at you. Her Nun name is Sr. Bernarda but she lets us call her by her regular person name. Even Mom's crazy about her, except when she gets mad at Dad cause he always likes things fixed extra special for Aunt May. Everything has to be sparkling, the furniture, the glasses, our shoes, even the car, Dad'll spend the morning polishing Gorgeous George while Mom runs around inside fixing our clothes and cooking and making sure she has her Best Irish Linen Tablecloth and Napkins on the table. We use the good dishes and knives and forks and the cut glass salt and pepper shakers and Mom puts out the white towels with the pink roses in the bathroom that are only for Show.

Mom'll make roast beef and mashed potatoes or Leg of Lamb with the Roasted Potatoes and string beans. And maybe tapioca pudding with raisins and cinnamon which I'll make and of course Mom's special peach upside down cake and maybe even her homemade vanilla ice cream. And there's always a little Blackberry Brandy that Mom takes out just for Aunt May. I always thought it was a sin for a Nun to have whiskey but I guess it isn't because Aunt May would never do it if it's a sin. Lots of things about Aunt May surprise me like the bubbliness and our cousin, Hugh Baxter having a party for her Feast Day in his Bar. Sometimes she even brings a girlfriend, Sr. Josephine Claire who's tiny and plump and jolly too and almost as fun as Aunt May and a really great cook. She's Italian she says. One time she told Mom not to cook and she made us the best Spaghetti and Meatballs we ever tasted.

Anyway, Aunt May always spends a whole day at our house laughing and eating and drinking Blackberry Brandy and going for a drive with Dad in Gorgeous George to see all the pretty houses in the Country Club section. And she brings Presents, in her drawstring bag. A little while after she gets here, she'll be drinking her tea and we'll be waiting but not saying a word and all of a sudden she'll open the bag and pull out chocolate Santas or Easter Bunnies and lace hankies for Mom and holy pictures and blue crystal rosaries and scapulars. And St. Christopher key chains and Holy Water from Lourdes and even once a wallet with a picture of Pope Pius and bookmarks and a bracelet and Miraculous Medals on sparkling silver chains and all sorts of great stuff. And not only holy stuff either, even Yo-Yos and Spauldings and purple and red kerchiefs and tablecloths she embroiders herself for Mom. Aunt May's a sixth grade Teacher and the kids in her class always bring her presents which she says we can put to better use than she can. And she always has enough for each of us to get two or even three presents.

The other good thing is that Aunt May's Tall. Almost as Tall as Me! And she acts like she thinks it's pretty great cause she always walks with her head and her back real real straight and not for a second ever looking like she wants to be normal size. And she says we're almost the same!

So I feel really bad that even though all that good stuff happens in Aunt May's life which for sure means you <u>can</u> still have fun and maybe even Adventure if you're a Nun, I still can't make myself want to be one. And I'm afraid her feelings'll be hurt and maybe she'll even be insulted if I decide I don't want to. Not only will I be disappointing Jesus and Dad who for sure deserves to have at least one of his kids Enter the Religious, it would be a Great Blessing, he always says. I worry that he's embarrassed in front of all the other men in the Nocturnal and Holy Name especially Mike O'Donnell cause his daughter Louise <u>is</u> going in. I wish I could not be so selfish and do that for Dad, it would be the Best Present in the World. For Aunt May too, she's sure I'll be a Nun just like her. You'll follow in my footsteps, won't you Suzie? she always says smiling that big puffy faced smile that's so great and makes me feel all warm and glowy. And I love it that she gave me a Nickname, bouncy and bubbly Suzie.

Aunt May even thinks Sonny'll be a Priest. I think she's the only one besides Father Jordan and Father Murphy, the priest in charge of the altar boys who expects Sonny to be a Priest. Dad just says if it's God's Will and if He does decide, it'll be a blessing, but Aunt May's sure. She says someday Sonny's going to be a Monsignor, a Priest who's a Boss and she's so sure that she calls him The Monsignor. And even though I get mad at him a lot, it kind of makes me happy for Sonny that Aunt May's so crazy about him.

Kay

unt May doesn't have a nickname for Catherine. She just calls her by her regular name which is the same as Dad's and Aunt May's Mom, Catherine Cusack. That's probably why Aunt May didn't pick a nickname for her cause she already has Aunt May's favorite name and why Daddy likes her so much that Mom thinks he loves Catherine more than her. Anyway Catherine's lucky cause The Crowd calls her Kay, Kay sounds older and rocky and less Goody Two Shoes than Catherine. I wish I could do something with Joan, it's kind of flat and boring and dull like a blob of cold mashed potatoes. It sure doesn't make you sound pretty or interesting, having a name like Joan's faggy like wearing oxfords. And what's really sad is that Mom says I'm named after <u>her</u> Mom who died, her name was Siobann. It's true, Joan in Irish is Siobann, it starts with sh like Be Quiet then a little v and the end rhymes with fawn. Doesn't that sound interesting and graceful kind of like a big beautiful bird taking off? Of course I think you have to be pretty mature if you're a girl to like that name but I do and I think I am, mature I mean. But it doesn't matter anyway cause Mom changed it to make it dull boring old Joan.

Beanstalk

I just saw Joyce walking towards the ball field. Probably to see if Sonny and his friends are still down there playing stick ball. She's always following them. I wish I didn't have to see her cause everytime I do I feel bad. See Joyce is the only other girl who's even close to my size. She's real skinny with Big Flat Feet just like mine. But her Mom doesn't buy her good shoes, Joyce goes by herself to Miles or Kitty Kelly at the Square and buys size 10s which're the biggest size they carry but she has to force her feet into them. And she sure doesn't know that girls with big feet should never wear white shoes. I don't think her mom's telling her what're the right things to wear and that white shoes make your feet look Huge.

Mom takes me to a Special store, Footsavers all the way down town for mine. Size 11 <u>Quadruple A!</u> Of course those stupid salesmen always have to remind me. When I tell the guy that the shoes he showed me are for old ladies and kids don't wear fat heeled grey suede pumps or tan oxfords, he'll say You know you happen to have a big foot young lady. He'll be so dumb squatting there lacing those stupid oxfords telling me I have big feet like this is news to me. And it's always so great how Mom lets me talk back to him like I'm the grownup. Oh really? I'll say, Thanks for telling me. Then Mom'll grab her pocketbook, get up in a huff saying, Well then I guess we came to the wrong place, and looking over at the manager standing smiling by the elevator, she'll raise her voice even louder, I was prepared to buy my daughter several pair, three or four maybe but I guess since you can't help us we'll have to go to Coward's where I'm sure they'll be happy to fit us.

It's true, even though I don't want it to be, sometimes Mom's mouth embarrasses me like when she yells at Tony the vegetable man that the potatoes are soft or when she told the bank manager she'd change banks after they bounced her check to Mr. Wrenn but when it comes to standing up for me with those stupid salesmen she's great. Of course the manager'll be over in a second asking what the problem is here and he's sure they can help me my feet aren't that big at all why they carry women's sizes up to 14. Then I'll start feeling sorry for the first guy, he'll be running back and forth bringing out all kinds of shoes calling them Youthful Styles meantime keeping an eye out for the manager to see if he's watching. I always worry later that he got in trouble after we left and lost his job and maybe he has lots of kids and no money for food or Christmas presents and I hate it when that happens, me worrying about him. But it seems like every time we go to buy shoes, there's a new guy and the old one's no-where around so I end up feeling like it's my fault. But bad as I feel about getting him fired and his family going hungry I forget about all that the next time some dumb salesman tells me I have big feet. Then there's the problem of the money. We don't have much and my shoes cost a lot cause believe it or not mine are also Flat. But Mom never complains about the money. You can never pay too much for good shoes. You only have one pair of feet, she says.

But not Joyce's Mom. And she doesn't teach her about hair either, Joyce has long stringy hair that looks like she never washes it, it just hangs there looking ugly. I'm lucky having Mom who used to be a Beautician so I learned about hair from watching her fixing mine and finger waving her own. I've gotten so good at doing hair that I have a bunch of my own customers, everyone's so crazy about how I fix hair. And Joyce doesn't have an older sister she can count on either to teach her stuff.

And Joyce I guess doesn't learn by watching other people like I do. Like what they wear and do you like it. I want to get real good at deciding for myself how things look, stylish or frumpy and stupid or pretty and glamorous or ugly and babyish and if I like them and think they'll look good on me. But Joyce doesn't seem to learn anything about rocky or not rocky or pretty or ugly by watching people so she doesn't even know how bad she looks. Which is probably good. I feel really sad about Joyce. She has no one teaching her anything like how to not walk around looking ugly like she doesn't know a thing about dressing and feeling like a girl. I learn by watching people's faces too. Their mouths tell me right away if they're laughing cause they think I'm a Giant or cause they like me and not even noticing how Tall my stupid body is. Or I can see a mouth and know it's mad even if it's not yelling and the lips are a scar like Mom's when she's mad the worst way. Or Dad's when he's thinking you should be Ashamed of yourself for hurting Jesus who Suffered and Died for Your Sins.

But Joyce isn't learning anything from kids faces either and that's a Huge Problem. Kids look at you alot when you're tall as us and laugh too and you never know what the laughing really means. All the kids think we're a Joke but Joyce is always trying to hang out with Sonny's gang thinking she fits in and they really like her and that's why they call her Struntsy and Beanstalk. And I'll be mad at her for being so dumb letting herself look so awful wearing those cheap stretched out flats size 10 scuffed white fake ballerina slippers. And you can see the bumps on her toes through the leather and the way the back of her foot stretches the shoe even further so her foot's practically out of it.

And I hate it that she lets the boys see her all hunched over hating what she looks like and wanting to be smaller and laughing when Sonny or Jimmy call out Hey Stretch! How's the Weather Up There? And inside my chest'll be burning that she's letting them know how bad she feels even though she thinks she's fooling them. There's nothing worse for a Too-Tall girl than letting the boys know you're trying to look small, that's like begging them to like you and acting like they're these really Important people and you care a whole lot what they think of you. And I'll be mad and hurting too for her almost believing they're her pals when they're laughing their brains out when she walks past. I'll want to be looking away my eyes not wanting to see her, she's ugly and hurting and burning inside like I am but sometimes I'll be forced to see her face which I think might even be almost pretty if it wasn't ruined completely by the mousy junky hair and her head hanging down from always trying to hide. But I can see inside her so I know how much she hurts like something in-side her is broken her face so sad no one can hide a feeling that bad everyone knows you're Ugly you do too you can see their faces Laughing at you looking like an Octopus a Giant a Big Clumsy Gawk you're Uglier than anyone ever so why <u>does</u> your Mom buy you beautiful clothes like it's not even a com-plete waste of money when you're this Huge Beanstalk with her legs so long they're flopping all around and you're bigger than anyone Big as your Dad so why waste the money Mom there's no way anything can make you feel beautiful and even the nice ones can't help laughing you look so bad and it burns all down my chest and belly that Joyce wants to walk around looking like a Dope pretending that's not true

And one time last summer I got really mad at that new lady Mrs. Bubell who just moved into the O'Connor house behind ours. We were both hanging out the wash and we said Hello but nothing else because I guess we were a little shy. Then she started calling her kids Billy and Sissie to come in the house to start their homework but when they didn't answer, she started to get mad and then she said it, These kids'll drive me crazy! (it seems like all the Moms are worried about that). How many do you have? Cross my heart that's what she said <u>How many do you have?</u> I was really mad at her thinking I'm already a Mom and old and me just trying to be a kid. It was weird and I knew it was because of the stupid Tallness. Anyway I answered kind of loud <u>Lady, I'm only Eleven! I'm not even Married!</u> She was real sorry and said so and asked if I wanted a babysitting job so of course I forgave her. It's not her fault if my stupid body wanted to look like it was fifty when it was only eleven.

Shopping

Oh who cares about stupid tallness. I like thinking about Saturday which was totally great. Mom and I went shopping downtown for my new winter coat. See I have two coats, one for Sunday, that's the new one and one for everyday, that's the old one. We found a really great one, blue like the color of dungarees with big wooden buttons and a nice shawl that you can flip right over your shoulder. It's so great. Mostly we shop before school starts and Easter, and we always have a pretty great time taking the train to Macys or Bloomingdales looking for really great clothes for me like hats and toppers and shoes and everything. And Mom teaches me all about clothes like how to tell whether the dress is well made or not and if the fabric's good. But not Catherine. Catherine has no taste at all, Mom says cause she's always shopping with her friends instead of Mom and spending her own money that she makes from working at the Five and Ten. So she buys clothes that look Cheap Mom says and don't show off her best Features which means her face. Mom likes it a lot that I never even <u>think</u> of shopping with anybody else except her and it's really too bad that Catherine doesn't cause it's true that Catherine's clothes <u>do</u> look kind of cheap but mine <u>never</u> do. Still I wish Mom didn't say mean things about Catherine to me. It makes me feel like a bad sister. But probably she's only saying it cause she figures I can keep a secret.

Mom's

Yesterday I heard Mom talking on the phone to Aunt Eileen who got married last summer and now she's having a baby. And Paddy who she married has a big huge family with about a million brothers and sisters and Mom was saying to Aunt Eileen to be careful cause when Catherine was born Dad's family like Aunt Rose and Aunt May Took Over the Baby and then they did the same thing when Sonny was born. So when I was born Mom said this one's mine and she didn't let anyone get near me, she kept me for herself. But I don't think I want to be only Mom's. I want to be everybody's.

A Complete Slob

Lucky for me Catherine and me don't have the same kinds of problems as Sonny and me. I guess cause she's a girl. She's even tall too and kind of flatchested so she knows how bad you can feel about yourself if you don't like what you look like and everyone around you is calling you names. Catherine never teases me. The only big problem we have is about our room, she always has her bed made with no wrinkles in the sheets or the blankets, she makes it so the bedspread's always smooth and never lumpy like mine.

Catherine's just the neatest person I know. She's so neat she changes her school blouse <u>every</u> day and for sure you don't have to, you can definitely get away with at least two or three days, two if you're <u>very</u> clean, three if you're more normal and four, once or twice even five if you're desperate and a Slob like me. But who cares? with the stupid uniform you wear the same stinking blouse every day. And Catherine changes her bra and <u>slip</u> every day too! Who changes their slip every day? how's it going to get dirty? For sure it's not going to get smelly cause it never hits your armpits where the BO is if you ever have it which Catherine for sure never does. If you ask me the only thing that has to be changed everyday is my underpants and that I'm pretty fussy about. Except every once in a while when I run out and have to wear the same pair twice or even three times. That makes me feel pretty weird specially if I have to go through all the dirty clothes in the hamper to find one that isn't too smelly.

This stuff's kind of private but I'm only talking about it to show how clean Catherine is and how she doesn't have to be. And she takes baths everyday. Who takes baths everyday? how's your body supposed to get dirty? I think a nice sponge bath where you wash under your arms and <u>down there</u> is fine. But for sure I take a regular one on Saturday night, we all do so we're nice and clean for church on Sunday.

Mom gets really mad about the room too. It's not that she minds that I always have huge lumps in my bed even after I made it and put the bedspread on, but she doesn't like the clothes under my bed and piled on top. Mom'll come in the room sometimes and throw everything off the bed and onto the floor then she'll open my drawers and dump them too. I was going to say she'll dump them if they're messy but they always are so it just never happens that Mom opens my drawers and doesn't dump them. But I just can't seem to care that much, it just seems to be a waste of time hanging up my clothes when I'm going to have to put them on again later or on Tuesday maybe or Saturday. When it's time to go to bed I'll just move them over just enough for me to have room to get in. It's true, sometimes I'm sorry the next morning cause my uniform's all wrinkled and for sure I'm not going to school with my uniform wrinkled and the pleats all messed up so I'll have to sneak downstairs to the cellar where the ironing board is without Mom noticing me.

But I wouldn't just make a <u>ball</u> of my uniform and throw it on the bed, it's more like I lay the clothes on the bed. It's just that by the end of the week there's alot of them and they're starting to get buried and wrinkled from all the other clothes piled on top, then if I want my sweater and I haven't worn it since Sunday maybe and this is Friday and I'm late for school so I have to pull it out like those tricks they do with tablecloths, everything'll come down in a huge lump and just my luck Mom'll come in yelling You'll be late for school! and she'll see the mountain and it'll be awful and that's when she gets the maddest at me.

Even Dad

There'll be no Christmas in this house, Mom says. She's in one of her Not Talking But You Don't Know Why Moods. I know I'm not supposed to be talking about this cause Mom always says Never Tell Anyone Outside What Goes On Inside Our Four Walls. It's like a Commandment and if you break it you commit a crime against the family. But I'm not, I'd never tell anyone, I'm just writing it in my own private notebook that's only for me. That way I can get it out of my brain but still keep it a total secret. Like Mom says we have to. It gets really confusing though, what you <u>can</u> say and what you <u>have to</u> say and what you <u>can't</u> say. Like anything that's good and nice you can say to anybody but anything's that's bad like sins or bad thoughts you have to say to Father in Confession and any problems or anything Bad about the Family you're Totally Completely Forbidden to say. That's Mom's Commandment. And none of us in a million years would even <u>think</u> of breaking it. So I'm really lucky to have my notebook.

And it really is true, Mom always gets mad at Christmas. Thanksgiving too. I mean she still cooks the turkey and shops with Dad for presents but no matter how hard we try she'll still be saying she can talk til she's blue in the face. It's too bad, I mean for sure we'll have Christmas but it would be so great if she could be all happy and bubbly like us and we didn't have to always be scared of her.

Even Dad's afraid to do anything that'll make Mom mad at him. Like when she tells him when he comes home from work about us being so bad we're driving her crazy. Daddy usually doesn't think anything we do is bad except if he catches us Lying maybe or Taking the Lord's Name in Vain which none of us in a million years would even think about doing. Or Gossiping about Our Neighbor. But Dad just doesn't seem to care too much if we put our clothes away and did we finish our spinach or potatoes and did we wash behind our ears and take our cod liver oil. That's stuff only Mom thinks about. But Dad thinking we're not so bad really gets her upset, she'll start crying that he's taking our part against her. He'll be saying that he just doesn't agree with her but she won't listen she'll be feeling like he doesn't love her if he isn't mad at us too. She always acts like they're supposed to feel the same way about us. I remember one time I think I even saw tears in his eyes cause Mom was saying he didn't really love her if he was taking our part. I felt really awful to be seeing Daddy crying, he was really really sad like he was so hurt inside that she would feel like that. After that I think is when he stopped saying he thought she was wrong, I guess he didn't want her feeling sad anymore or that he maybe wasn't a good husband.

Nicknames

Even though Catherine's the one Mom gets mad at the most, Daddy never does. He has his own special name for her, Bobba. It's a nice pet name that makes you feel like she's still his baby or his little girl. Dad usually doesn't call me by any other name but Joan except every once in a while he calls me Pet which feels all Warm inside. Sonny's nickname stuck so much that lots of people don't even know his real name's Eugene just like Dad's. Dad even has a nickname for Jerry, Little Joe. But he doesn't have a Pet Name for Mom. Unless maybe he whispers it cause it's a secret. He always calls her Mom and she calls him Dad, except when we have company when they call each other Gene and Mary. Or when Mom's Mad at Dad, she calls him Gene then too. Dad never gets mad at Mom so I don't know what he would call her if he did.

I just thought of something, about names I mean. Not nicknames just regular names. Maybe cause I'm named after Mom's Mom, I <u>am</u> Mom's Favorite like Sonny always says and maybe cause Catherine's named after Dad's Mom, she's his favorite so maybe even though they're not supposed to Play Favorites with their Own Kids maybe Mom and Dad really do. And I feel kind of funny about that cause I think maybe I'm not so completely crazy about being Mom's Favorite.

Pretty Girl Presents

nyway I don't think Mom has to feel bad if Dad doesn't have a pet name for her cause one thing he for sure does is buy her Beautiful presents. I wonder what he'll get her this year. Last Christmas he saved all his leftover carfare money and hid it under the leg of the kitchen table and bought her a Watch all gold with tiny but still very sparkly Diamonds on the side. It's a Hamilton Mom says. Mom never had anything that beautiful before. And Dad buys her Chanel No. 5 <u>real</u> perfume. And even No. 21, the kind in the tiny velvet box like they put rings in. I'm always really Happy for Mom that Dad does that even though she doesn't wear it much cause she keeps it for Show or for very special things like a wedding maybe or her kid's First Communion.

The True Christmas Spirit

om and Catherine aren't the only ones who get great presents from Dad, I do too. Like for Christmas I got my Two Wheeler, a Schwinn all blue and beautiful with lots of silver and even tassles coming out of the handlebars. We already know that Santa isn't helping out at all so each year only one of us gets a big present which we're completely dying for and some small ones too and the rest of us get just small ones. And that's really okay cause you can't be Selfish always wishing it was you getting the big present, you have to share in a family and besides you always know for sure you'll get your turn someday. Anyway it was almost Christmas and all of a sudden the Magic Skin Doll was invented. I was really dying to have one, you could give her a bath. Mom didn't find out I wanted one til Christmas Eve and she says she told Dad when he came home from work at 4:30. It was snowing so bad it was almost a Blizzard so the buses weren't running but Dad <u>walked</u> to Parkchester to Macys to buy me one. He walked four miles down and four miles back from Edgewater to Parkchester in the freezing teeming snow! And I hope Catherine and Sonny and Jerry didn't get mad thinking that I was the Favorite maybe getting <u>two</u> special presents. We all had to wait til almost 9 o'clock to even get our tree cause we always wait for Dad to do that, up til then is Advent and you're supposed to be sacrificing and praying all the time getting ready for Jesus to be born so for sure not celebrating.

Dad always says it isn't right people getting trees and colored lights and Santa Clauses and jolly cards with snow and sleds and reindeers which are all Pagan symbols he says that miss the whole point that it's the Lord's Birthday so the only thing we should even be caring about is the Manger and celebrating that Jesus is coming and the celebrating should be praying and Mass and <u>Religious</u> cards not Pagan Symbols. And for sure we shouldn't be acting like Advent's over and it's already Christmas when it isn't. So we always have to wait til Christmas Eve night to get our tree. Which if you're being selfish thinking about the wrong things being important you might even say is too bad cause it means we can only get a pretty stinky tree, all skinny and no nice fat branches but it's Christ's birthday not ours so who cares if we have to wait a little and get a really scroungy tree that Dad always has to chop the top off of so he can get it in the house. And so what if it's even a little embarrassing when your friends come over on Christmas to see your presents. Things like how big your tree is or how fat and how many branches it has shouldn't matter if you have The True Christmas Spirit, that means you really don't care about anything even presents except thinking and praying about Jesus being born.

Anyway this Christmas was even worse cause because of me we had to wait even later to get our tree which meant it was the worst ever. Catherine and Jerry and even Sonny didn't say anything about it being my fault though, they just seemed really Happy for me that I got my Bike <u>and</u> my Magic Skin Doll so with Mom and Dad being so Great about presents and Catherine too everyone ends up really happy. Even Mom even if it's only for a little while.

Boys and Girls

Catherine's so cool. I wish I could hang around with her like we were Girlfriends and maybe someday even be her Best Friend, but probably not, people would be thinking you're Hard Up having a younger sister for your friend. One thing that's really great though is that she and her friends like to talk about their boyfriends to me. It's really weird but even though I never had a boyfriend I kind of know what you should do and what you should say and what you should wear and how you should act around a boy and how you should never in a million years let him know you like him cause once he knows you're finished. Only when he asks you to Go Steady and he gives you his Senior Ring can you tell him you like him too cause if a guy thinks he can get you to like him in two seconds for sure he won't like you. And guys only like girls that all the other guys like. These are some of the things I tell Kitty and Frances and Catherine when they start liking a guy. And I think then that Catherine's proud of me and glad I'm her sister, I know for sure that's one time I feel like I'm just as old as them and for sure not a Snitcher.

†

JMJ

Snitcher

Sometimes you have to do things that make you feel funny, like following your brother and sister home from school. It's my job Mom says to watch where Catherine and Sonny go so I can tell her, that way she can stop them right away if they're doing things that're bad. It's for their own good so I'm really helping them she says. I don't feel like that though, I feel like a Traitor. But Mom found out that Sonny's smoking and Catherine's going to Joan Jenkins house for lunch and even going there sometimes after school instead of coming right home so Mom needs to know <u>each</u> time they do it so she can punish them and make sure they don't do it again. But I'm not always sure what's so bad about that stuff, except maybe the smoking. And we have to be careful about the kids they're hanging around with too, she says to make sure they don't end up with Big Archie or Willie Leonard and Georgie Scase, they're the older guys that quit school at 16 and spend all their time lifting weights and drinking beer and Making Out at the beach Friday nights with girls in black sweaters buttoned down the back.

Anyway I think Catherine and Sonny have really started to hate me, no kid's supposed to tell on another kid specially to their mother even if they're mean and tease you a lot. I asked Mom if I could please not do it but she says I'm the only one she can count on and it's for their own good she keeps saying so I have to be her Spy. Otherwise I'll be committing a sin against the Fourth, Honor Thy Father and Thy Mother. And now they're saying I'm the Favorite and Goody Two Shoes and when I come in the room, they stop whispering. They tell each other lots of secrets. Even their friends know about me Snitching so everyone stops talking when I come around. And Sonny made me swear I wouldn't tell anyone I'm his sister, he doesn't want me embarrassing him and if he finds out I did, he'll <u>punch</u> me he says. Sonny can get pretty mad when you don't do what he tells you to. And if I tell Mom he says I'll <u>really be sorry</u>. I told him everyone already knows I'm his sister but he says just in case I meet a new kid like that guy I met on the bus who asked if I was Cusack's sister, I'm supposed to lie and say I'm not but I <u>can't</u>.

Lying

I'm really really careful about Lying. It's a sin anytime you do it even if it's about something like did you finish your homework or do you like that boy. And Lying can slip pretty fast from a venial but not too too bad into a Mortal which is Awful. And you're always Guilty cause you always <u>know</u> you're Lying. A Lie can't just happen even if it slips out by accident because once you say it, the Lie I mean you have to say right away, That's not true. Then there's the problem of knowing for sure what's a Really Serious Mortal and what's a not so serious venial. You can't take any chances cause supposing you mistook a Serious for a not so serious, you could be Finished like Hell I mean.

But that's where God steps in to help us out, He knows we don't want to hurt Him but we're human so we're forever committing sins. And that <u>does</u> hurt Him. But He forgives us. That's why He came up with the idea of Free Will and Conscience, that's the part of you that knows what a sin is. But He knows that sometimes the Conscience can slip up so He says for a sin to be Mortal we have to <u>want</u> to commit one, you have to know how much it hurts Him and still decide to do it. So if you think it's Mortal it is, even if it's supposed to be venial and if you think it's a venial it is even if it's supposed to be Mortal. That's Free Will. It's so nice of Him bending the rules like that. Still it's not fair to take advantage, you should only count on Free Will and Conscience in a huge Emergency, you should always be trying not to do <u>anything</u> to hurt God and that means not committing sins ever. But you know some'll slip in anyway, specially sins against the Fourth and Lying, so I figure to protect God's feelings the best thing is make sure not to say <u>anything</u> I can't be sure is <u>totally completely</u> true. But hard as I try when Mom or Sister ask me something in that deep scary This Is Serious voice, I don't believe myself anymore and even though I don't remember doing anything I know I <u>must</u> have been bad.

Did you do it?

No.

Are you <u>sure</u>? Answer me! Are you <u>sure</u>?

Well I <u>think</u> I didn't do it.

But maybe I just <u>think</u> I didn't and I really <u>did</u> so I could still be lying. Or maybe I just <u>think I thought</u> but I didn't really think so I just <u>think that I thought I thought</u>. See how you can never be sure you're telling the truth so you need someone <u>outside</u> to tell you what the truth is. That's what Sister does and Mom.

Nervous

So I couldn't pretend that Catherine and Sonny weren't doing anything bad so there was nothing to snitch about cause that would be lying so a Mortal. And even if I could lie which I totally can't, Mom would know anyway. Mom knows everything even when she's maybe a mile away and she'd kill me when she found out, totally completely kill me. See Mom has lots of ways of getting Mad. All scary. Like when she won't talk to you forever no matter how much you beg her and you don't even know what you did but you say you're sorry anyway but she still won't talk to you, that's the worst way. And no one else'll talk to you either cause then they'll get in big trouble too. So you're all by yourself in the family. Then maybe in an hour or a day or a week, all of a sudden Mom says give me a kiss right here pointing to her cheek and you know she's not mad anymore. First all Mad, then the Kiss and Not Mad. And it's true you're so happy she wants to be talking to you again but you don't like the Kisses you don't know why but you don't want to kiss her but what's the Big Deal just one little kiss and everything's good again so you do.

Another way Mom gets mad is when she yells and maybe even screams and then she'll grab The Belt which she always keeps close by. Once she got so mad at Sonny she hit him a bunch of times with the iron cord. When Mom gets mad that way at me and takes out The Belt and comes after me yelling Get in here! my whole chest and arms up to my shoulders and down even to my belly'll get all shaky and trembly and I won't be able to even breathe and I'll be almost peeing in my pants and begging and crying I won't do it again Mom I promise Please don't hit me I'll be good I promise I promise I'll be good I promise. So Mom's afraid I'll have a Nervous Breakdown if she hits me, I heard her telling Catherine or maybe Sonny when they were saying it isn't fair that I never get hit and they always do. I feel pretty guilty about that but it's not that I'm faking cause I'm not. Then sometimes in the middle of the shaking I'll get even scareder and that scared feels all black inside my chest and head cause this time I'm sure she'll do it so I have to shake more to look more Nervous so she won't. But sometimes I'm not sure if I'm shaking more to <u>look</u> more scared so I really <u>am</u> faking or if I'm shaking more cause I <u>am</u> more scared so I'm not faking.

Even though for sure I'm scared of the beatings I felt a little bit good when Mom got so mad at me one day she grabbed the strap and started hitting me and yelling Maybe this will stop the shaking! If you won't stop it, the belt will! Of course that's not the kind of thing a kid would feel even a little good about I know but as bad as it is at least it doesn't add to the hating thing with Sonny and Catherine cause if I'm getting hit too even though I'm Nervous which might even mean my beating's a little <u>worse</u> than theirs, not cause of the whacks but because of me being so Nervous, then maybe I'm not the Favorite so they won't have to hate me for it. Me getting beaten too means we're the same, Catherine, Sonny and me. And when he's old enough Jerry'll be part of this too, getting beatings I mean.

Twins

Soon as the Snitching started the teasing got really bad specially from Sonny. But it isn't the first time he hated me, I think he hated me from that time he took me in the closet and cut off all my hair, I was four and he was five. I don't remember it but Catherine does. Mom too. Sonny and I used to be like twins Mom says, always doing everything together. I'm not sure if he wanted it that way but Mom wanted it so that's the way it was.

All the girls think Sonny looks like James Dean and he does, I swear it specially since he started sleeping with that nylon stocking over his head that makes his hair all smooth in the back and bushy on top like James Dean's. And shrinking his Levis in the bathtub, it's a trick he has where you put on your dungarees and sit for hours in the bathtub in hot as you can stand it water. For sure he'd kill me if he knew I saw him. Anyway there's no one rockier to look like if you're a guy than James Dean. So that makes me a little popular with some of the girls, they like hanging around with me so they can be around him too.

Sonny's only eleven months older than me, he's 13 Catherine's 15 and Jerry's 9 so we're right in the middle of the family. Mom always says we look alike and because I'm tall for my age and he's kind of normal and our hair's the same color and kind of wavy in the back, we look like twins. So when we were younger, Mom started treating us like we really were and had us watching out for each other in the street or at the beach or in school. I guess that way she could pay more attention to Jerry who was the baby and needed her more than we did. And I liked having a built-in friend.

The first thing that happened, the one I don't remember was that Sonny took me into a closet, the one in Mom and Dad's room that later became the Dining Room. Catherine told me he sat me down on that old trunk Mom keeps in there filled with mothballs and blankets and pillows and old flannel nightgowns that you never want to wear cause they smell so bad from the mothballs. When I picture going in there it feels so nice sitting there all warm and cozy with Mom's dresses all around me and Sonny laughing and holding the scissors saying It's time for a haircut. The way everyone talks though I think I'm supposed to feel really mad or even scared like he's doing something bad to me. Mom says we really looked like twins when Sonny got finished with me, even our hair the same length. I had the Most Beautiful Hair she'd ever seen on a child Mom says, lots of fat long curls down almost to my tush that Mom washed and rolled in rags every Saturday night for Sunday Mass. All the old ladies admired them she says, til Sonny gave me the haircut.

And when we were growing up I had to teach him to tie his shoelaces and later he had to teach me to ride my bike. Sometimes he really got mad cause he wanted to ride with his friends instead of me and Mom said No when he asked her couldn't I just follow along behind them but Mom said he'd forget all about me. One day he was so mad he took the Dirt Road racing ahead of me standing bobbing left and right I got so scared trying to keep up, I fell off and got a huge hole in my knee. I walked the bike the rest of the way to school and had to report to Sr. Mary Bernard, the Principal to explain why I was late. I tried to hide my knee but she noticed me limping I guess and called for Sonny from his classroom and told him to take me home to get it cleaned and bandaged. I knew he'd start hating me right away, Mom would be mad and asking questions and blaming him for not watching me and riding too fast and he'd be in Hot Water again.

It's true, every time we do something together, he ends up getting in trouble or having problems. Once he needed a haircut and Mom decided he was too big for her to cut his hair anymore so she sent the two of us and told me what to tell the barber. Sonny was all excited about getting a grown-up haircut until that stupid barber started to laugh at him and said, What's the matter kid you need your sister to take you for a haircut? Of course Sonny hated me, he wouldn't even talk to me, he walked home ahead of me and the next time he needed a haircut he told me over his dead body I'd go with him. So I just met up with him at the corner and walked home with him. That barber ruined everything for us.

†
JMJ

The Meanest Nun I Ever Knew

But Sr. Mary Antonio did something a million times Worse. Which I maybe shouldn't even be talking about cause she's a Nun but I'm just explaining about me and Sonny and him hating me. Anyway, I think this might even be a Mortal. It's true, she's the meanest Nun I ever knew with a huge moon face and tiny eyes that're like slits with big puffy bulges where her lids should be. And her sleeves are always rolled up and pinned like she has Serious Business to take care of.

Anyway Sister hated Sonny when he was in fourth grade. I always thought it was a sin to Hate someone especially for a Nun but she was so mean to Sonny that Mom and Dad didn't blame him when she got mad at him and I think Jesus probably agreed with them. Then one time she called for Mom to come and see her, that meant he was really in Hot Water and this time even Dad went so you knew it was Serious. We were all so scared that Sonny was really going to get it when they came home because Nuns're <u>always</u> right, everything they say God agrees with, everyone knows that. Mom always says Don't ever come home complaining that Sister's wrong when she blames you for something because you'll get in more trouble when you get here. The amazing thing this time though was that when Dad and Mom came home that night they weren't even mad at Sonny <u>and</u> they said they'd buy him a bike if he could just get through the year without any red marks in Deportment. None of us ever knew what happened in that meeting but we all figured Sr. Mary Antonio must have been so Mean and Nasty that even Mom and Dad couldn't accept that as doing God's wishes. Nobody, not even a Nun gets away with bad mouthing Mom's kids so I figure Sr. Mary Antonio mustn't have realized who she was dealing with when she started telling Mom how bad Sonny is. After that things were pretty peaceful between Sonny and Sister.

Then one day Catherine Cavanaugh, the Brain of the Fourth Grade came in to Sr. Mary Gerald's third grade with a note asking for me to come up to Sonny's class. I got really scared, the last place I ever wanted to go was Sr. Mary Antonio's room. All Sonny's friends were in there and they laughed at the younger kids and whispered when we came in the room, specially me being so Tall. When I got there Sonny was standing at the blackboard next to some numbers that were scribbled over and Sister was yelling waving the chalk and banging the ruler on Jimmy Flood's desk <u>I said, what is six times six, Eugene?</u> Sonny was getting all blotchy and red around his face and ears the way he does when Dad gets mad the kids all blur faced and frozen Sister suddenly turned slitty eyes popping yelling

JOAN! What is six times six?!

36

LOUDER! Six times seven?!

42. All of a sudden I had to pee real bad.

Six times eight?!

48.

And she wouldn't stop just kept yelling questions bang-ing the ruler Mary Whatshername in the back row jumping a little with each bang.

And what is 6 divided into 72? 8 times 7? 9 into 81? <u>Prove it!</u> Write it on the board!

<u>Eugene!</u> Watch what she's doing! Explain it out loud so we can hear you!

WoolieswetSqueeze!Squeeze!Harder!!

9 goes into 81 9 times HOLDIT!9 times 9 is 81.

Heads down the boys by the window all snickering but this time it's not just me they're laughing at it's Sonny too and Sister's yelling in that mean talking through her teeth slow and spitty way Aren't you Ashamed that your third grade sister has to teach you Math?! <u>Answer me Eugene! Aren't you Ashamed that your younger sister has to teach you Math ?!</u>

That Scary Laugh

I was really scared to go home. I knew Sonny'd be waiting for me. He called me into Mom's room that's now the Dining Room. I came right away cause I'd never not do what he says and Sit down I want to talk to you he said. Where's Mom? And Catherine and Jerry I said and he was laughing that scary laugh saying Mom's out shopping and Jerry has softball and Catherine's waiting for him so it's just you and me Snitcher. I was trying real hard to not care what he does and not be scared cause who does he think he is he can't scare me but all of a sudden I had to pee real bad and he was yelling Get Up! Why? I said Just Shut Up and Get Up he screamed but when I did he jumped at me with his teeth all hissing and spitting the veins in his neck all red and popping his arms flying out and smashing my chest throwing me down on the bed Get Up but this time quiet and slow like he's ready to punch me I tried to say no but my mouth wouldn't let me it was frozen and he was yelling louder GET UP I SAID then he was flying at me again his hands like big brooms his mouth huge and open howling oh yeah oh yeah where ya goin snitcher and he smashed me down again onto moms mattress with the springs squeeking and me bouncing my legs and feet flying and trying real hard to hold it scared this time he won't stop he'll make me pee Please let me go

Just let me go to the bathroom but that made him laugh even louder and Come On GET UP! DO IT or you'll get even worse I was shaking inside praying Please Lord Please Lord Save Me! muscles popping in his arms his eyes wild like a tiger a crazy dog and this time he'll kill me UP I SAID GETUP!! Please Sonny I'm sorry I gotta go to the bathroom can I please go GETUP and SMASH UPSMASHPLEASE UP SMASH I have to go SMASH but I just couldn't squeeze any longer and I Peed all over myself through my Woolies and my uniform down to my socks and onto Mom's bed and he was laughing his brains out pointing to my uniform where my privates are that were all wet and Mom's bed too and he was choking his stupid head off and then it was over he just walked into the kitchen and opened the fridge he didn't care about me any-more. The game was over and he won he made me pee and when I think about that now I really really DO Hate him even if it is a sin

We were Finished after that. Now I stay away from him as much as possible cause when he's mad he laughs that Scary Laugh and you know something Awful's going to happen. It's weird about Sonny, when he gets mad he doesn't yell and say he hates you, he just laughs so hard and so loud that his face gets all Red from the laughing and that's when the veins in his neck'll go all blue and start popping out like they're ready to Burst and you know any second blood'll be flying all around all over the furniture and who knows what'll happen to him then or me

Sonny's Games

I keep worrying that I'm breaking Mom's Commandment cause all this happens within our four walls but sometimes I have to say stuff. It just flies out of me. And even though I don't Talk about it, I only write it in my notebook and nobody knows I even have one and for sure I'd <u>never TELL</u> anyone this stuff even Catherine or Jerry or Marie and for sure not Mom and Dad, Mom probably still wouldn't like it. But it's true, my Big Brother's a Bully. He totally hates me and I'm totally scared of him. He's always ready to pounce on me. Like kill me I mean. I wish I could disappear when he's around. Now everyday after school it's always the same. Sonny orders me and Jerry into Mom's room and stands at the door laughing that Scary Laugh of his and playing that Stupid game of Throwing Us Down on the Bed yelling that we have to try to get up and get past him so he can knock us down again and if we don't he says he'll <u>really punch</u> us and that'll for sure be worse. But it's funny about Sonny, some games he plays more with me than he does with Jerry, like the Knocking You Down on the Bed Game he plays much longer with me than Jerry. He lets Jerry out after only about 7 or 8 throw downs but he always takes a lot longer to be finished with me.

Another of Sonny's games that's just for me is the Turning the Lights Out in the Cellar When I'm Down There Alone Folding Laundry Game then making weird scary Devil sounds and turning them on again then hiding under the stairs moving his hands round and around making monster shapes on the ceiling then howling and turning out the lights again and I'll be shaking and screaming and crying for Mom or Jerry and I won't be able to move like I'm paralyzed and of course I'll be peeing all over myself again and feeling so ashamed like a Big Gigantic Baby. And that's not the only thing Sonny does to me, sometimes he even gets Jerry to play too. At the breakfast table. Sonny says he doesn't want to have to look at me when he's eating and he doesn't want me breathing on his food so I have to sit at the end of the table and not talk at all to him or even look at him. He puts the Cheerios box in front of him and starts reading it but sometimes he can still see me over the top or the sides so he'll get the Corn Flakes box and the milk bottle and even a loaf of bread and build a huge wall. Then he starts reading the boxes. If I talk even in a whisper to Catherine or Jerry he'll say he can still hear me and to Shut Up if I know what's good for me so I do but still I'll move my mouth saying the words with my lips sending silent messages to Jerry who stopped playing a lot earlier.

Usually I'll just be laughing the whole time like it doesn't matter one bit and I don't want to talk to him either but no matter how hard I try down deep inside myself he does win. I totally hate that and I almost want to lie and say to myself that he doesn't but I can't. It's hard to not feel bad that somebody you know, somebody in your own family even if he is your Big Bully Brother thinks you're so Disgusting you ruin his food just by looking at it, and even though you'll pretend that you don't even hear him or care one tiny bit what he thinks it <u>does</u> make you feel kind of Ugly and Awful looking, here's your brother who's a boy thinking you're so Ugly you make him Sick.

I wish Sonny was afraid of Mom, or even Dad, but I don't think he is. I mean if Mom really scared him then maybe he'd stop all his Bullying. But maybe he just knows that me and Jerry won't run and tell on him when Mom comes home. He never bothers Catherine cause she's older and they have secrets. He just saves up the meanness for when Mom and Dad go out or when they're really really busy with the laundry maybe or paying the bills or praying. As soon as they're not looking, Bingo! Sonny's Mean and you can't yell or cry or call Mom or Dad cause then he'll get you even worse and you always know that if Sonny says he'll get you for sure he will.

Jerry and Joan

nyway, with Sonny and Catherine hating me, I needed a friend too so I took over Jerry. And what was really great was that he needed a friend too. See he was real upset when he had to go to school and leave Mom cause he had spent the most time alone with her. After that he used to fake Double Headaches and stomach aches so he could stay home. Of course he didn't say that was the reason, no kid'll admit that they get sick so they can stay home with their Mom specially if the kid's a boy. Sometimes Mom tries to trick him to see if he's really sick by telling him that he can stay home but that he has to go shopping with her to Hearns Basement. Now there's nothing Jerry hates more than shopping with Mom so if he says Okay then she knows he's really sick. And Jerry hates it when Mom goes out, even though she hardly ever does except when she goes for a ride with Dad on Saturday afternoons or up to our cousin Hugh Baxter's maybe for corned beef and cabbage every once in a while on a Thursday night.

Anyway Jerry has a really bad temper and when Catherine can't get him to stop yelling and screaming, she'll lock him in the Back Room which we think of as the Beating Room cause that's where Mom always hits us and she'll tell him she won't unlock it til he stops screaming. That makes him really wild and he'll start kicking the door, once he even punched a hole in the wall. Now it might seem like Jerry's this wild and nasty kid kicking and screaming and punching all the time and maybe even a Bully but he isn't, he's really nice except if you're being Mean to him. He's all soft inside and he gets scared easy like me too. He's very cute with a bunch of hair sticking up straight in the back of his head and his face is like an Angel's, beautiful and soft.

And Jerry really thinks I'm smart and nice and not a Joke. I understand him cause we have lots of the same feelings like wanting to be close to Mom and make her Happy but sometimes being Scared too. And we're both scared of Sonny of course. Nothing feels better than Sonny being nice to you except maybe Mom being nice. When we first started being friends we used to follow each other around, one sitting on the tub while the other was on the toilet, we liked to pretend we were Mom and her friends. Even though she says she has no use for girlfriends, Jerry and I liked to pretend she has lots of them and we took turns playing her and the friends we chose for her. And when Mom sends me down to the Cellar at night to bank the fire or to hang up laundry I always bring Jerry with me. And he never laughs at me for being scared of Monsters. Even though he's younger and a lot smaller than me I'm not so scared if he's there, even if Sonny's down there making his Monster shapes on the ceiling and walls.

Jerry and Sonny

Even though Sonny's mean, Jerry's pretty crazy about him. But I don't think Sonny even likes Jerry. And I don't know why cause for sure Jerry's not a Snitcher, but maybe Sonny hates Jerry cause Jerry likes me. And as bad as it is for me having Sonny playing jokes on me, it's even worse for Jerry. Every night after the lights're out and Jerry's almost asleep, Sonny'll whisper Jerry, are you asleep? Jerry's always afraid of what's next. Sonny'll keep talking I know you're not sleeping so don't try to pretend. Watch out cause before you fall asleep I'm going to punch you five times.

You don't scare me Jerry'll say. He likes to pretend Sonny doesn't bother him but Jerry's Scared to Death of Sonny. Sonny's Mean and he's been <u>lifting</u> weights, he hides them in the cellar so Mom won't find them and he has Huge Muscles. The only thing for Jerry to do is stay awake so he can see Sonny's fist coming and move away just in time so he won't get punched. But sooner or later Sonny'll fall asleep and I guess he'll snore or breathe real heavy or Jerry'll throw something on the bed or the floor and Sonny won't move, but that doesn't happen for hours, long after Mom and Dad go to bed. I feel so bad for him having to be scared every night. And sometimes Sonny <u>does</u> punch him and real hard too so Jerry never knows when it's coming and Sonny says if Jerry <u>flinches</u>

when he's punched he'll get another harder punch. That's always the rule with Sonny, if you fight back even a little you get it worse. But Jerry and me don't fight back, we can't stop Sonny. Nobody can stop him.

Like What Lucifer Did

With Sonny driving me so crazy, I'm having trouble Loving Him as Myself. And I'm not doing too great with the First Great Commandment either. I can never be sure if I'm loving God with my <u>whole</u> complete heart and my <u>whole</u> soul and my <u>whole</u> mind and with <u>all</u> my strength. And of course the Soul part really confuses me, but I figure if I could get the other three the Soul'll probably be included. Still for sure I'm failing at the whole mind parts especially with some of the Bad Thoughts I've been almost having. It's true, the hardest part of taking care of your Soul is Controlling your Thoughts cause Thoughts are Sins if you have the wrong ones. And Bad Thoughts ruin your soul too just like Disobeying your Mom and Eating Meat on Friday so you have to do everything you can not to have them. I mean God wrote down the rules in the Commandments, all we have to do is do what He says and be Thankful to Him for our Life and Everything. I'm pretty good at that part but sometimes all of a sudden I'll be thinking of something that's a sin, like not being so completely happy about going to Mass or almost getting mad at Mom or hating someone like Sonny or wishing I didn't have to kneel for the Rosary.

But the Problem's even worse when I'm worrying about Purgatory and the Burning, like thinking maybe God could've made Purgatory a place right outside Heaven, like a vestibule in Church but no Fire. For sure we'll be suffering just by not being able to see Him and not being in that great place that Heaven is with Him and the Angels and Martyrs and the Blessed Mother and St. Joseph. But telling God that putting fire in Purgatory wasn't so great was a really bad idea so I pushed it away fast and buried it with four Our Fathers so it was gone right away. But I knew it had been there and God did too, it had come from me and it hurt God and I was afraid I had sinned, maybe even a Mortal cause I think this one for sure was Pride. Lucifer's Sin. Telling God how to do His job for sure would be a Mortal, nobody ever knows enough or is holy enough so they can tell God they aren't crazy about the way He's doing things.

And I can never figure out when a thought <u>becomes</u> a sin, I mean is it a sin from the beginning just because I thought it even if only for a second? Or do I have to let the thought come in and stay for awhile? And for how long?

God's Favorites

t Mass on Sunday Father was saying we don't have enough priests and nuns, specially Cloisters. So he needs us to pray for God to choose us. It's really hard to pray for that though. I'm scared that God already decided that He <u>does</u> want me and to be a Cloister too. See there are two kinds of Nuns, Regulars who teach us in school and watch us at Sunday Mass and Cloisters who we can never see and who never do anything but pray, like the Poor Clares. So they pray all day and night except for a few hours off for sleeping on a cot with no mattress. Or maybe a straw one or just raw wood. And no covers except maybe one really skinny blanket with holes in it like the kind Baby Jesus was probably wrapped in cause that's all the shepherd's had, old holey blankets they used for the cows maybe when they got sick. Or the sheep or maybe it was the goats. Anyway I figure it's probably very good for the Poor Clares to be a little bit cold all the time cause the Baby Jesus probably was. But Nuns don't mind, they even like it cause it's another chance for a little Suffering and Poor Clares spend <u>their whole life</u> sacrificing for God. They don't want another thing in life but to be with God thinking and praying all day and all night so they couldn't care less about talking or laughing or listening to the radio or getting new clothes. They probably even <u>love</u> it when their knees hurt from all the kneeling. They don't even listen to music but they all have good voices, I hear them at Mass in the Monastery. I love the high holy sound of their voices singing and me kneeling beside Dad. And when the Poor Clares stop singing all you can hear is Father's voice saying the prayers and the beautiful sound of the Sisters saying the parts that the altar boy usually says.

I figure Cloisters must be God's <u>Most</u> Favorite, not only His favorites among humans but Nuns too. They never do one single thing, not even one small tiny thing that doesn't have to do with Jesus, and praying. There isn't even anything that they ever <u>want</u> to do or that they even <u>think</u> about that isn't about Him. But of course humans, even Cloisters can never be perfect. Let's just say they're as perfect and holy as any human being can be except maybe for the Martyrs who had their Heads Chopped Off or were Eaten by Lions or Burned at the Stake. They let themselves go through all that killing cause they loved God so much. I wish I could want to be a Martyr cause that would be proof that I love God as much as possible. But I'm scared I won't be able to, I'll be too Weak. So I'm kind of glad I don't have to walk around living during a time when people get killed and turn into Martyrs just for loving God. I feel bad that I'm so scared of all that hurting and torture that maybe I wouldn't be strong enough to take it, I don't think I'd want to live anymore if I turned out to be the kind of person who worried more about pain and her own life than about standing up for God. And not only could I never be a Martyr but I could never be a Cloister either. Even if I wanted to be which sad to say I can't make myself want to, for sure they'd never accept someone like me who can't keep her mouth shut join the Cloisters. What makes me even more Ashamed is that in a way I'm almost glad. I feel bad that I'd always be thinking about going outside or saying something to my neighbor and not maybe about God. I can't imagine ever loving God so much that I could give up living outside and talking! I wish I was so good that I'd <u>love</u> giving up talking for God and everything else too but the almost glad part means maybe I'm Safe I won't have to be a Cloister It makes me so Ashamed all Weak and Ungrateful inside to say that but I have to It's Terrible but it's True so I have to say it and I can't imagine God ever getting over that I'm scared that I'm really Breaking His Heart this time

Giant

ven though there's about a million Problems I'm always worrying about, I think the Tallness is the Biggest. Except maybe for the Controlling My Thoughts one. But sometimes I get really really Scared my body might want to be a <u>Giant</u>. See we learned in school about how the different glands control things. Like the organs and stuff. First I really paid attention when Sister started to talk about the Pituitary because that's the one that decides how tall you're going to be but then when she started explaining about Giants, I tried not to hear how everything gets huge even their feet and their Ears and I was getting really really Scared. And now I can never forget about the Pituitary even though I try to. It's the gland I don't trust like I don't trust my kidneys not to want to pee all the time even when I just did or there's no toilet around, it's like that with my Pituitary, I almost hate it and Sister says it's this little itty bitty gland that's so small you'd never expect it to be so Important.

And today the worst thing happened. Sister measured us. I hate being measured, in school or at Doctor Green's. I wish I could've gotten so sick I had to stay home so I wouldn't have to hear Sister call out how tall my Stupid Body got. But Mom never lets us stay home. My belly was really hurting like burning almost and I had to pee every two seconds and I was praying and praying Please Lord I don't want to hear it let her forget don't let her say it don't let them hear please Jesus don't make it much I CAN'T BE TALLER please Jesus I'm Tall as the chart that has lots of numbers for what's normal in boys and girls and what's normal for girls even <u>boys</u> at 12 isn't what I am I'm not even normal for a <u>boy of 16 or 17</u> when an almost 6 foot tall boy is still above average and for sure there's no such thing as an almost <u>6 foot Tall Girl</u>. Please Jesus Help me. But Sister was saying Joan stand against the chart, straighten your back head up everyone real real quiet Sister yelling so the whole school can hear <u>5 FEET 11 AND A HALF INCHES</u>! then the snickering everyone thinking it's a riot Sister yelling QUIET! I SAID QUIET! Stop your snickering it's black inside my head they're right it's a joke my huge Gigantic body that's grown two more inches No one's this TALL almost peeing the fire in my belly get to the bathroom please Jesus help me

I never told anyone about being scared my body's planning to be a Giant but when the sleeves on my coat're so short my sweater hangs down and Mom had to buy me a new one even though she bought me one last year and none of the other kids need new ones every year, I start thinking it really will for sure happen. And Sister says sometimes a Giant just happens cause the System's Weird and I for sure know my System's Weird, it already decided to be Nervous, have really bad belly aches and give me Big Feet that're also Flat and Pee more than any other kid or human person around so maybe it's also planning to never stop growing. People always say that girls don't stop til they're 18 and I hate it when they say that cause I'm only 12 and I'm already <u>5 Feet 11 1/2 Inches!</u> and I'll never let anyone say I'm 6 feet tall cause I'm not and all of a sudden my whole body has the burning in it and the terrible pains in my belly and I have to go to the bathroom and I'll be lying there on the floor for a long time til the pains go away and I can finally get up I don't think I can live if I'm a Giant Huge like a Tree my arms and legs flopping all over like a Giant Octopus getting paid to be a Freak in the circus everyone gaping and pointing and laughing like there's no bigger Joke than you

NO WAY!

Even if I <u>am</u> a Giant, I'll <u>NEVER</u> take a job standing still in the Circus letting people Laugh at me.

Big Brothers

ast Friday I slept over my best friend Marie's house. She has <u>three</u> big brothers, Raymond, Richie and Georgie and I'm really really Scared of them. They're almost Men, they don't go to school anymore, they work. Georgie scares me the most, he's loud like Sonny and his hair's always greasy and sticking out in places it's supposed to be lying down. And his clothes are greasy and his fingernails too and he wears big heavy black Boots that scare me every time I hear them stomping up the steps. And I'm always afraid he'll hit me, he never does but he likes to tease me, not cause I'm tall but he says I talk funny so I'm always kind of mad when Georgie's there cause he ruins everything. Raymond though is a little nice when he's by himself and Richie's really nice but when they're all together it's almost like they're one Mean Person.

Anyway, Friday Mom let me go to Marie's as soon as I got home from school and that was so great. Well, Marie and I were having cookies and pretzels and Kool Aid and sitting on the floor watching First Love when all three Brothers came home together and all of a sudden I was Scared just like that. But I didn't show it of course. They were all out in the kitchen banging the fridge and opening Ballantine beer bottles by smashing them on the side of the counter, then

they were coming into the room where we were to play darts.
We couldn't even get away from them, their voices getting
louder and Louder and them Laughing and Howling and
starting to kick beer bottles out of the way so I figured they
were getting Drunk like always. And Georgie was <u>Cursing</u> of
course which I totally hate and taking the Lord's name in
vain like he didn't even care and they were moving round
and around almost in circles and I was praying real fast to
myself of course Hail Mary Full of Grace the Lord Is with
Thee cause I thought for sure something really bad was going to happen and then it was Georgie's turn and he tripped
over Raymond's boots and cursed and started flashing his
dart in the air back and forth at me and Marie as if any
second he'd throw it and hit us just like that and we'd be
Dead. And he was laughing real loud then all of a sudden
he turned real fast on his feet like he was a dancer with his
eyes real scary flashing and red at the corners and wide open
like he saw something that scared him and he was pointing
at me and howling laughing Come here Miss Irish Girl now
it's your turn. Show us what you learned in school! And he
was Huge standing over us still on the floor me almost peeing and my face all burning and all of them dragging their
chairs in a circle around us and throwing their huge boots
out in front of them so they were pointing straight at us aiming like arrows almost and Georgie was shouting Stand up
Irish girl stand up! Tell us! What letter comes after G? And
they were screaming laughing each time I said it screaming
at the sound of it

H

Louder!

H

LOUDER!

H

And Georgie was pounding his fists and banging his huge
boots on the floor and they were falling down laughing and
choking having Convulsions and I didn't even know what was
so funny but Marie said later it was funny the way I said H
just like Mom does and Dad, which I thought must be a sin
laughing at someone just for the way they talk and I almost
hated them for being so mean and scaring me cause I'm just a
kid and they're just Bullies and I never did anything to them.
I really wanted to go home and never come back but Marie
begged me not to and Mr. Vogel came in and gave me a big
Hello like he was really happy to see me and I went to pee and
decided that stupid Georgie and Raymond and even Richie
weren't going to make me leave when this was the first time
in a long time I got to sleep over. And anyway they were all
going out after the ball game and probably wouldn't get home
til tomorrow anyway.

Later at the dinner table though they all turned around to
watch me, even Marie and the Mom who started to act kind of
mean too when I made the Sign of the Cross and said Grace.
In our house we always say Grace and Dad says that when
you're in someone's house where they don't say it, you're supposed to say it to yourself. Which is what I did. But as soon as
I started to make the Sign of the Cross they started to laugh I
could feel my face getting all red and I hate that and I thought
it had to be extremely bad what they were doing making fun
of someone saying Grace. Then the mother was asking me to
have some meat and I didn't know why she was asking it, I
never met a Mom who tried to get you to do something you're

forbidden to, she knows it's against my Religion to eat meat on Friday and she said she'd have some fish sticks for me instead of the meat and here she's saying have some chicken. No Thank you I said I don't eat meat on Friday but then Georgie was opening up his Big Mouth again and I was really really Hating him saying Come on Who's gonna tell? Just one little piece and he was leaning back making the muscles in his chest pop up and down and he wasn't even wearing a shirt and he was watching them like they were really something great til Mr. Vogel was saying That's Enough like he really meant it. After dinner they sat around listening to the ball game and all three of them fell asleep and were snoring real loud so it was hard for Marie and me to hear the TV. And there were lots of beer bottles standing on the floor in a line like soldiers. I was glad when they finally woke up and went out cause that was the end of them for that night.

Anyway, its true, Marie's Mom is kind of mean too, almost like she's a kid. Sometimes when I'm feeling pretty Great cause I'm wearing a new outfit Mom bought me for Easter or maybe my new coat, Mrs. Vogel'll say the color doesn't go with my face. I've heard of colors that don't go with your eyes or your hair but never colors that don't go with your face. What kind of face doesn't go with a blue coat? And one time when she saw my grey tailored suit, she said it was too old for me and she'd never let Marie wear a style like that. But Mom thought it was great and so did the saleslady. I totally loved it and felt very elegant except just a teeny bit self conscious cause that's always there but when I saw Mrs. Vogel, she made me feel a whole lot Self Conscious and my belly started Burning. A lot. And I was starting to not like the suit. She made it sound like Mom was being a bad Mom for letting me wear it so I was feeling kind of mad at her for saying that, and even though I didn't want to a little bit mad at Mom that maybe she was letting me walk around looking like a Gawk in ladies clothes. Of course if Mom knew she'd say that Mrs. Vogel was just Jealous cause Marie doesn't look like a Model so she can't wear sophisticated clothes, and I try really really hard to believe that. I feel sorry for Marie having a Mom and three brothers who're so mean, and I feel bad for Mr. Vogel too. And even though I don't think I want to go back there, I can't just <u>flat leave</u> her cause of her Creepy Stupid Brothers but I can never tell Mom what happened, she'd never let me go back to Marie's house again.

And besides Mrs. Vogel changing from nice to mean, she doesn't seem to even care about her house being clean and looking like a nice family kind of place. And besides the stupid dart board, the Vogels living room has a lot of things in it that seem weird. Like stuffed animals on the wall, a deer's head and a huge grey fish and a squirrel standing on the bookcase behind Mrs. Vogel's chair. And they still look real like they'll jump right out at you any second. And there's the great big brown coal furnace. I mean we have a furnace too but not in the Living Room! Ours is in the cellar where it's supposed to be but the Vogels don't have a cellar. And the Dad's even a plumber. And in the living room you're supposed to have couches and pictures and lamps with ruffled shades even if they have to be plastic and if you're lucky even carpeting. But in the Vogels there's <u>linoleum</u> on the floor! In the living room! And only standing lamps that are also ash trays by Mr. and Mrs. Vogel's chairs and a couch that has dogs running on it and wooden arms with ash trays filled with cigarette butts and a small table next to it with a deck of cards and a lamp that's really a big brown jug with whiskey signs on it. And there's no nice tablecloth or matching pretty dishes and the ketchup and mustard and jelly jars are always on the table even when they're not eating. But still even though the mother and the brothers are hugely Mean to you, you wouldn't in a million years let yourself even think about making fun of them and their house saying it's Ugly cause of how much it would hurt Jesus you being so Uncharitable not Loving Your Neighbor as Yourself, even though they for sure aren't loving you as themself.

A Dirty Pig

E ven though they almost did, the Vogels didn't make
me pee. Just almost. But I was really scared that they
would and then they'd NEVER stop laughing at me,
even the Mom. Maybe Marie too. See The Peeing in My Pants
Problem's a really Huge one, I try to pretend it's no big deal
cause I'm so ashamed but it is so I have to say it, I still wet the
bed. Every night, or almost. And I'm in 7th grade! First Mom
thought it was my kidneys and I couldn't help it. That's what
Dr. Green told us but then she started acting mad and making me wash my sheets every day before school. Sonny thinks
that's a Riot. I guess she figured that would make me stop but
it didn't. No matter how much I hate having to wash those
stupid sheets in the bathtub every morning in the freezing
cold water kneeling on the freezing cold floor I can't stop.
Finally she took me to Dr. Rossi, this kidney doctor that Mrs.
Vogel told her about. Not that Mom ever let on to Mrs. Vogel
about my problem, but she listens to Mrs. Vogel talking about
her own troubles. Mrs. Vogel always has Troubles, not only
with the boys quitting school and Georgie and Richie having
to get married and Marie being kind of fat and Aunt Peg and
Uncle Frank drinking so much. And for sure she must worry
about those awful blue runny sores she has on her legs. I try
not to look, I know how bad you can feel with somebody gap-

ing at you like there's something really Weird about you. I can usually pretend they aren't there specially when she wears those thick brown cotton stockings that're so ugly, but they hide the Ulcers, that's what she calls them. But sometimes she doesn't cover them and I try not to notice but my eyes want to keep sneaking a peek, a few times she even saw me. It's hard though the way she sits right out there in the middle of the living room with her legs bare, you try not to but you have to see them.

Anyway as soon as I saw Dr. Rossi the kidney doctor I didn't want him touching me. He's not like Dr. Green. When we were little and even now if we want them, Dr. Green gives us lollipops when we go to see him. And he has a nice round face like a cake almost with normal eyes and no hair on his chin only neat thin glasses with frames made of real silver. And he doesn't think it's terrible either me wetting my bed. He just looks from Mom to me every time she mentions it and touches my hair and says, She'll grow out of it. She's just nervous. But Mom was getting tired of waiting so she decided to take me to a Specialist. I didn't like Dr. Rossi as soon as I saw him, he's scary looking with those squinty eyes and that skinny moustache and a body that starts out kind of small, at his shoulders I mean and then gets bigger and bigger til it's huge where his belly button would be. And then it starts going in again and gets smaller and smaller til it ends in the tiniest feet I ever saw, like Humpty Dumpty.

I like the way I sound all cocky and sure of myself when I talk about him cause that's the way I wanted to feel, that I wasn't all scared and crumbling inside. Anyway he examined me I guess, I can't remember that part, only the part of first seeing him and maybe a little bit scared and wishing he'd smile and peeing even a little right there on the table before the nurse handed me the bottle. I don't remember anything after that really except what he said was a very big deal cause he told Mom and she told me and later Dad that I'm just a <u>Dirty Pig</u>, it was really awful and I really hated him even though Jesus wants me to Turn The Other Cheek. He acts like I <u>like</u> wetting the bed, like I'm not even hugely embarrassed every time I wake up in the morning with those stinking sheets all twisted and smelly and even the blanket wet and me freezing and my nightgown wet and up around my face and even my hair stinking. And I suppose that creepy doctor thinks I like it when I have to drag those stupid sheets through the kitchen every morning while everyone else eats breakfast, Sonny complaining to Mom he can't eat with the Stink and sleeping on that stupid rubber sheet that makes those loud crackling noises every time I move in the bed so Catherine and even Sonny in the next room can hear it. When I wake up in the dark in the middle of the night alone and freezing I'm afraid to move, if I lay totally stiff no cold air can get in and make the wet sheets even colder but even one leg shifting will start me shivering again and needing to pee but I can't get out of this bed it's so cold

And when do you ever stop feeling like a baby and start feeling like a girl? And how can you ever feel pretty and have a boyfriend when you still wet your bed? Will I be wetting when I'm 16? What if the other kids can tell cause I smell from pee like I can tell the Murphy kids still pee in their beds cause wherever they go you can smell pee.

But I still didn't say the totally worst thing that ever happened. I wish I could make it not true but I can't and it is so I have to say it I even peed in my pants once <u>in school</u>, right there in the class room. In 6th grade! See I had to go a lot that day and you always have to ask Sister if you can and some-times she says no. It's embarrassing to ask anyway in front of the boys, they all think it's a riot, the girls having to pee. I tried to hold it cause I already asked twice that day and Sister was getting mad and the boys were snickering again which is the word Sister uses when they're not supposed to be laugh-ing cause they're in school or in Church or it's mean and Sister'll for sure get really mad if she catches you and make you eat your lunch in the classroom all by yourself. And you won't be able to play stickball with your friends so you have to close your mouth real tight and cover it with your hand so you don't get in Big Trouble with Sister.

The only one who wasn't laughing was Tommy Dunphy, Tommy never laughs at me, I think he even likes me. Just as a girl. I know I really like him and as a boyfriend too but I never let him know, he's so much shorter than me. Boys don't like girls that are taller than them and I'm afraid he'd laugh at me for sure this time or at least want to. But anyway I was holding it and squeezing real tight and it's almost lunch time concen-trating on arithmetic squeezing my legs pulling in hard down there Please Jesus! Please help me! Please hold it! and all of a sudden Sister dropped her book on Jimmy Garvey's desk and pee was gushing sloshing making a puddle under my desk I wanted to die it's a sin I know but I still wanted to there was no way out I could never get up from that desk or be seen by anyone in that class again and I still don't understand what I did that made God let that happen

Jesus, Are You Mad?

ear Jesus, Please don't be mad at me. I'm scared You are and that's why You didn't answer my Please Don't Let Me Pee Prayers. Maybe You're getting tired of all my bad thoughts wishing I didn't have to go to Mass or kneel for the Rosary and sometimes hating Sonny. I'm really really Sorry I'm always hurting you. I try so hard but I keep messing up.

But maybe You're <u>not</u> mad but God just wants the peeing in front of everybody to be part of my Cross, so I can suffer a little like You did being crucified for my sins. So I'm sort of helping out. Please Jesus, let that be true.

My Friend

ut one thing Jesus took very good care of that day was Sr. Mary Callista, she was really nice to me. Usually she's very strict and mad a lot and fat with chubby cheeks and a really huge chest. But that day she excused the class early for lunch as soon as Jimmy Garvey discovered the puddle and started pointing and snickering. She found me in the lavatory, I ran in there as soon as the class emptied out. She acted like it wasn't the worst thing in the world me peeing all over myself and the floor in front of the whole 6th grade specially that creep Jimmy Garvey who'd probably already told Sonny and the other 7th grade boys who were for sure howling and laughing their stupid heads off. Tommy Dunphy would just be feeling sorry for me and that's worse than anything. So I said okay when Sister tried to convince me to leave the girls room and even think about coming back to class the next day, but she understood that I wasn't making any promises.

Sister even started talking to me about private things, just the two of us like girlfriends almost standing close together there in the girls room in front of the hissing spitting radiator talking about private girl things that Mom doesn't like to talk about too much like My Friend which I hadn't gotten yet but was hoping for very soon. Any day now, Dr. Green told Mom when she took me to see him about the stomach aches I was getting every month, so it wasn't Appendix like Sonny said but My Friend getting ready to start. I couldn't wait, Catherine was <u>16</u>! She just got it this year and I was scared the same thing would happen to me. When the others girls said they couldn't go swimming cause they had their Friend, she had to Lie and say she couldn't either cause it's extremely embarrassing to be 16 and not have your Friend. So I was lucky and very proud that mine was on its way when I was only 11. Really 11 and 3/4. I was worried that that would cause problems though between me and Catherine but lucky for us hers came two months before mine, she was so happy she didn't seem to care that I almost beat her.

Anyway I did go back to school the next day. I for sure want to go to College so there's no way I could quit school in the 6th grade. Besides Mom and Dad would never let me go to Public School, who knows what they teach there? You could lose your Faith. And I don't even know how I got myself there except I do remember a lot of softness that day like wearing Catherine's pink sweater over my uniform, it was really nice that she let me. Sonny even walked me to school and didn't tease me like when we go to Mass in the summer. I like it that I don't remember any teasing that day, but I can't really be sure, sometimes I remember things that I want to be true. And Sister picked me to be Second Grade Monitor saying she needed someone Responsible to help Sr. Mary Pauline who wanted a 6th grader to come down and watch the little kids while she went to a meeting, she's this tall skinny Nun with teeth marks on her lips like she spends her whole life biting them. I'm really scared of her. All the other kids raised their hands too but Sister just looked right past them and picked me. I was still wearing the pink sweater when I went down there and Sister was smiling and saying Thank you like what I was doing was real important and helped her a lot.

Anyway telling Sister about My Friend coming any day now seemed to smooth things over, in a weird way almost explaining my Accident, that's what Sister called it which I think was really nice. And lucky for me the first big thing that happened to me after my Accident was that I got my Friend. I was so excited I couldn't believe my eyes, none of the girls I know ever got their Friend when they were only 11. 11 and 3/4 I mean. Virginia got hers at 12 1/2 so I'm definitely the winner and it feels pretty great to be such a Success at such a girl thing especially after being such a failure with my flat chest and of course my height and wetting the bed. Being 11 and 9 months and getting your Friend is an extremely Lucky thing. But I didn't brag or anything, I just let them know I couldn't go swimming. It's the best thing in the world to not be able to go swimming cause you have your Friend.

Cross My Heart

he second great thing that happened to me after my Accident was that I saw Tommy Dunphy writing in blue chalk on the road Tommy D. Likes Joan C! Inside a Heart! Right out there in the middle of the road where anyone could see. He looked at me a little bit shy and I knew it was true, he's six inches shorter than me and even the guys my size think I'm a Joke so what could be nicer? And this isn't a memory I just want to remember. And it's not like I'm lying or pretending and making up stories so you'll believe me cause I'm not Cross My Heart everything I'm saying is true. I was wearing my blue shorts and that dumb Honor Roll pin on my peasant blouse which I still can't wear pulled down off my shoulder and my feet all bare and the tar starting to bubble up Cross My Heart It <u>Did</u> Happen.

The Nun Problem

But as soon as I start feeling a little happy to be a girl, I get all scared that I'll have to be a Nun. See one of the things I'm supposed to be doing to take care of my soul is praying for God to choose me for a Religious Vocation. Which means He picks me to become a Nun or a Priest if I was a boy. Nuns are married to Jesus. They even wear a wedding ring and you can still have a Wedding but the Groom isn't there of course. It's too bad that He isn't at the Wedding, His Body I mean but He's on the altar in the Host. But you can still walk down the aisle in the beautiful long white gown with maybe even a train. But sad to say right after the wedding part you have to take off the wedding dress and the veil and put on the long black frumpy Habit with the gigantic rosary beads hanging down and the black stockings and big lumpy oxfords. And the head thing, you have to wear it cause you can't show any hair if you're a Nun, I guess hair must be immodest like skin. I don't really understand why but I know a lot of Nuns and I never once saw one bit of hair, even Aunt May, I never saw a strand of <u>her</u> hair. Sometimes I try to picture it and I imagine it black and curly and long or red and maybe shoulder length in a flip. But it doesn't work. Finally me and Virginia and Catherine Cavanaugh and Frank De Mott decided that the hair must be shaved, there's no way that with all the Nuns we know that we wouldn't see just one little bit of hair if it was there, just one little strand that escaped but we just never did. I feel pretty guilty picturing the heads because of the baldness being so personal and for sure embarrassing for Sister or Aunt May so I try not to.

My favorite head thing's the one our Nuns wear, they're the Sisters of the Divine Compassion. Their whole outfit's pretty great, for Nun's clothes I mean. It has a really pretty black dress with big airy sleeves trimmed in red with a little ribbon of red around the front bib, then a wide cinch belt, four or five inches even and deep full pleats that go all the way to the floor. So if a Nun has a really small waist like I do, she can look like a Model for Nun's Habits. And it has a thin flowy veil like a bride's except it's black and it stays close to the face and isn't this huge thing like an airplane that some Habits have. Aunt May's is more like a big circle that starts at one shoulder and goes all the way round in a big swoop past the top of her head to her other shoulder like a huge halo. Maybe that's part of the Sacrifice you make being a Nun, going around for the rest of your life with this big ugly thing flying off your head.

I feel kind of sorry for the ones with the ugly habits. I can't understand why they didn't choose an Order that has a prettier Habit like our Divine Compassions. They're all marrying Jesus so why not do it in a pretty Habit? And don't they ever miss their clothes like their favorite poodle skirt or their Easter topper? And Nuns even give up their names. Even though I'm not exactly crazy about mine, I don't think I'd want to get used to a completely new name and not know when people are talking to me cause I'm so used to being called Joan. And what if it's an awful name that I wouldn't be caught dead having? Like Bertha or Gertrude, or maybe it's even a man's name like John or Stephen or Joseph! What could be worse than to be a girl with a boy's name. And getting up in the middle of the night to pray, even Regulars have to do that not just Cloisters. Being so sleepy all the time, having to pray in the dark kneeling on concrete and shivering from the cold when everyone else in the world is sleeping under their covers.

Obedience bothers me too, I don't think when I'm a grown-up I want to be obedient. I figure Obedience is supposed to end when you're not a kid anymore but that's one of the Vows that the Sisters have to take, plus Chastity which is okay with me cause I don't think I'd want to be doing that anyway. The other vow is Poverty which really isn't too bad either, it's true that I've always wanted a fur coat and my own spending money and of course a car but I can get used to it. It's not like I'm rich and have to give away all my money and my jewelry. Anyway God's great to me always giving me stuff like my bike and Tommy writing in a heart that he likes me so what's the big deal if I did have to give up my jewelry? But the Obedience Vow's the biggest problem, I'd be disappointing God all the time like I feel when I wet my bed so no matter how hard I prayed the night before I failed again. And I still don't know why God doesn't seem to hear my Please Don't Let Me Pee Prayers. Is it my Cross or is He mad at me? I wish I could be like the girls who want to be Nuns, they're so lucky they're in love with the Habit and don't care about having to be obedient and I don't blame God one bit for loving them more than me which I'm sure He does.

But sometimes I wonder if Nuns ever feel Jealous of all the other Nuns who're married to Jesus too. But that's really Selfish cause it has to be so great for Jesus having so many Brides loving Him more than anything, for sure that's what He deserves, Totally and Completely. But still I keep feeling that I'd want to be the Favorite and the Best, not wanting to share even. But probably not Nuns cause jealousy's a sin and Nuns don't commit sins.

Sap

om's really mad at Catherine today yelling about not liking her friends, saying they Take Advantage and Catherine's a Sap for trusting them. I don't exactly know what a Sap is but I know it's something I don't want to be called. I guess Mom's feelings are hurt that Catherine doesn't ask her advice on things, maybe she asks her friends instead. All I know is Catherine likes them a lot and likes going over to their house to sleep over so Mom says Catherine likes her friends houses better than ours. I don't know if Mom's right about that but even though Mom makes her favorite Creamed Fish on Fridays when the rest of us eat fish sticks or flounder and even though Mom never makes her eat peas which she totally hates, Catherine thinks she's Adopted. She's always asking Mom where The Adoption Papers are. I used to hope that she was just saying that to try to get Mom to be nice to her but I worry that she really feels that way that she doesn't belong to our family and the reason Mom acts like she's always mad at her is because she <u>was</u> adopted and we weren't.

Deep Down Inside Mom

I don't want to think about all this stuff and Mom'd probably be Hugely Mad if she knew I was even just writing about it but I have to cause I can't stop the thoughts from coming in and as soon as they do and they do a lot my belly starts burning really really bad so I figure maybe writing it can get it out of me the way talking to Father makes me feel a little better and even makes the sins seem a little bit smaller. I feel so so sad about Catherine and Mom. It's not nice to say and it would really hurt Catherine a lot if she knew but sometimes Mom acts like she doesn't even <u>like</u> her, and it seems like it wouldn't even completely break Mom's heart if Catherine ran away. So I'm really scared someday she will. I mean I know Mom would look for her everywhere, not herself maybe but she'd send Sonny and me and even Jerry and of course Dad. It's just that I'm afraid maybe Mom's heart wouldn't be jumping up all laughing and happy when she saw her. See Mom acts like everything Catherine does is bad, and it's true that Mom acts like that alot with Sonny too and even Jerry and me sometimes but it seems like it's a little extra with Catherine. Sometimes she acts like down deep inside herself we're not the kids she always dreamed of. Specially Catherine. And she'd totally KILL me if she ever found out I wrote about that.

Only Flesh and Blood

One thing that lets me feel a little bit better is that even though she has problems with Mom not liking her, Catherine doesn't have to feel <u>really</u> bad cause she's totally Cool having so many friends and being in The Crowd. And the Crowd is girls <u>and</u> Boys. They're the Rocky kids and they're all crazy about Catherine like I am and Dad and even Sonny, Jerry too and even though she isn't <u>Most</u> Popular, she's pretty close to the top. And it's not nice to say but I wish Mom would be more like Catherine and have girlfriends too but she says she has no time for them. I don't think that's the reason though. She says You Can Only Trust Flesh and Blood when she's telling us that our best friends should always be our brother or sister and not Some Stranger. But sometimes you just like your friends better and you want to spend all your time playing with them instead of seeing your brother and sister 24 hours a day even when you're swimming or playing ball or going out Trick or Treating. But Mom doesn't think it's nice if you have more fun with a kid not in your family. That's why she sometimes gets in one of her Not Talking to You Like You Did Something Bad Moods when your friends come over. She's just not too crazy about any of our friends. And I feel really bad about that cause sometimes I think Marie and Mary can tell that Mom wishes they didn't come over. And most times when I ask if I can have a friend over for dinner or sleeping over, she'll say we don't have enough room at the table or in the beds and even though that's maybe true, I still feel bad, I mean they could sleep on the floor or I could. Even though I try hard not to be I'm kind of ashamed that I have a Mom who doesn't like friends.

Irish

aybe it's because she's Irish and kids in Ireland are always so busy taking care of the cows they have no time for playing and friends. Mom and Dad came out here when they were old enough to work Dad says. Mom was first a maid which makes me really sad for her having to clean up everyone's mess but then she graduated to Hairdresser. Dad worked in the shipyards, then he went to Delahanty Plumbing School and became someone who has to take care of the pipes and the hot water and sad to say the toilets in people's houses. But Dad's smart so they mostly send him to big buildings like the Telephone Company and Con Edison instead of just houses and he's usually the Boss of the job.

When Dad goes to work, he carries his overalls in a brown paper bag under his arm. His Farmer Browns he calls them, which I guess is all they ever wore in Ireland. His lunch is in there too and his thermos of tea. I wish he had a regular lunch pail, black and metal and shaped like a little house except a pointy roof. Sometimes I even wish he'd wear Sunday clothes to work like he's really Important like the men who work in banks who wear suits and white shirts and those very serious looking ties and very polished brown shoes with the holes in the front. And they carry the newspaper under their arms and you know for sure how totally Important they are cause they carry a <u>Briefcase</u>. I wish Dad did too. And I wish he came home at 6 o'clock like Mr. Carey and the other Dads who work in offices not in the cellar fixing the pipes and the toilets with their knees killing them from kneeling all day on the stupid cement. And they get to sit down all day at desks and start work at 9 o'clock when we start school, not 7:30.

Even Marie's Dad who's a plumber too and comes home at 4:30 always comes home looking handsome wearing nicely creased pants like you'd maybe wear even to Mass. And a hat not a cap like Daddy wears, a regular one like you wear on Sunday so you can't even tell he's a plumber. Not like Dad wearing those faded plaid flannel shirts and grey Sears Roebuck pants that're so old the knees're almost white from Mom washing them maybe a million times. Mr. Vogel looks like Clark Gable all the grown ups say. Clark Gable must really be handsome cause that's what Mr. Vogel is. He likes to dress up all the time in straw hats and suits the color of vanilla ice cream and walk with a cane under his arm. And that's a surprise too, I mean the straw hats and vanilla ice-cream suits.

Sad to say, Mom doesn't care about her clothes either, only mine. She just walks around all the time wearing house dresses, the kind that old ladies wear that are buttoned up the front and have tiny tiny flowers on them. And lots of times they're kind of dirty on the belly like where it hits up against the sink or the stove or the washing machine and that makes me kind of embarrassed even though I don't want it to. But Mom and Dad just don't seem to care how they look. I figure it's because of them coming from Ireland and living all the time with cows and chickens and even pigs. But I wish Mom would dress like she thinks she's Pretty cause she is. Like in those pictures of her looking like a movie star in the sailor hat and pants. And the really long black dress with the high neck and long tight sleeves and the little velvet hat with lots of tiny curls peeking out making upside down question marks on her forehead and cheeks, her hands on her hips like she's a Model, Beautiful but not in a snooty way. And she's real real thin like a thin thin tree and her long dark dress is the bark. So I think it's about time that she got some new clothes. But she says there isn't enough money for everything and it's a Mom's job to take care of her kids.

It makes me feel pretty bad about myself thinking this stuff when I think of how poor Mom and Dad drove themselves Crazy doing everything for us. Sometimes I even wish they didn't come from Ireland and they weren't poor and wearing old clothes and saying some of their words a little funny. Like Haytch instead of just H like the Vogel boys said I do and a nice word like Certificate that Mom says really weird starting with the big sound Cer like Yes <u>Sir</u> then the other sounds real small til she ends with ayte like you <u>ate</u> your dinner so everybody can tell right away she came from The Old Country. I feel really bad like it's Mean and Snobby even but it's true, I would be so Happy if they were American.

That's the stuff I try to squish right away before it can pop up as a totally complete thought inside my brain. But sometimes it just doesn't work, the bad thought kind of screams inside your head and pushes out everything else. That's been happening a lot. Like thinking Mom <u>can't read</u>. I don't know why but I think Mom not being Smart would be the Worst thing for me to hear cause for me it's real real Important that Mom <u>and</u> Dad are smart. And we know for sure that Dad's Smart but lots of times we're scared Mom isn't, like I can't remember her ever reading something out loud so probably it's true that she <u>can't</u> read. Like it's not the kind of thing you'd learn if you're spending all your time as a little kid taking care of cows. So I never asked Mom to read me any stories or help with my homework so she won't be embarrassed. But sometimes I see the notes she writes to Sister when I'm absent and some words aren't spelled right and the letters aren't even and smooth, so Sister can tell from her notes that Mom maybe didn't go to school. I don't want to but I feel kind of ashamed of her and that for sure makes me really Ashamed <u>of myself</u>. I'm so sorry dear Jesus. And I know you heard me cause you hear everything even if I'm only thinking it. Lucky for me Mom and Dad can't hear me. Maybe I'll make them some tapioca for dessert, it's their favorite.

Purgatory

I can't stop worrying about Purgatory, like how much time I'll have to spend there. Of course I can never be sure I won't end up in HELL but I'm trying really hard. In Purgatory you get kind of cleaned up for Heaven but I'm still not so crazy about it cause you Burn there too. I used to hope that maybe God made the Purgatory fire a little less hot than Hell's so it doesn't burn as much, but I'm afraid maybe He didn't, it's just that it's not Forever.

But I've been wondering, if God made Purgatory and Heaven where He lives then where was He before He had a chance to create a home for Himself? The Catechism and Sister too says He <u>always was</u> which means He wasn't ever born, except Christ who was definitely born. It seems to me though that He had to <u>start</u> sometime like He wasn't here and then He was, but <u>always was</u> sounds like He was floating around forever until He started creating things. But then what about the place He was floating in, didn't He have to create that too? And where would He have been before He created that place unless someplace existed before Him? But He's supposed to be the first at everything. See how messy and confusing everything gets when you start trying to figure things out. I shouldn't be thinking this stuff anyway cause that's where Faith comes in, all I have to do is have Faith and just accept Whatever Holy Mother Church teaches, Sister says. You're not supposed to be asking any questions, it's not respectful to God. But sometimes I just can't help it, it just happens all by itself and it's stupid anyway cause the way Sister and Dad explain it humans can't understand, we're too imperfect and it takes a Perfect Brain like only God has to understand all this stuff.

†
JMJ

Tapped

ven if I'm not so crazy about being a Nun, for positively
sure I'll go into the convent if God taps me. I'll have to,
I just couldn't hurt Jesus by saying no. See I know He'll
surprise me, probably during Mass or Communion or Retreat
when we say the Rosary with long Litanies to the Blessed Virgin so the Rosary lasts for 30 minutes like at our house. And
Father'll get up on the pulpit and talk to us about Loving
God and Atoning and Giving Thanks and Avoiding the Near
Occasions of Sin like going to movies that have curses or too
much love in them or wearing tight clothes and a lot of lip-
stick or your hair pulled back and pinned behind only one ear
and the other side falling down around your face and wearing sweaters buttoned down the back or hanging out with
the Wrong Crowd. Or even not paying attention in school or
during your prayers because that's when Satan'll come in and
start giving you Bad Thoughts, Satan loves an Idle Mind Father always says, Sister too. So mine must be really really Idle.
And during Retreat Father always says There's nothing greater
or more pleasing to God than another young man or woman
entering the Religious Life so Retreat really scares me cause I
think that's when most of the kids get tapped. Of course I do
everything I can not to have these Wishing I Don't Have to
Go Thoughts like praying real fast when the thought starts to

creep in but I can feel myself getting scared when the tapped kids start telling everyone they decided to enter cause maybe I'm next, I get so Scared I start talking to Jesus to kind of distract Him but I know He knows, He didn't hear me <u>praying</u> for Him to choose me. That's what you're supposed to do if you really love Him the way He deserves to be loved. Christ lets Himself be Crucified for me and I can't even be a simple little Nun for Him. And I always figured Jesus only taps kids so once you finish high school, you're safe. But then Miss Clooney, our gym teacher was tapped and she has a Boyfriend and a Car and Nice Clothes and is even Pretty and all of a sudden, one day she says she's leaving her job to Enter the Convent! That means <u>you're never safe</u>.

Safe

ut one place I'm mostly always safe is at the Beach.
Just before supper when no one else is around. See
I <u>really</u> like quiet but I never get to hear it living in a
tiny tiny house with people yelling and screaming all the time
cause everyone in our house has a Big Mouth except maybe
Dad. But you <u>have to</u> yell in our house cause if you don't,
nobody'll ever hear anything you say. Even at supper Mom
and Dad have to tell us to be quiet and let someone else talk
cause you can't get a word in edgewise.

That's what's so cool about the beach, there are no voices.
No sound at all but the Quiet and the Water. The water isn't
in a rush and it likes where it is and what it's doing. I even
like the sound of its name, the Long Island Sound. Somedays
if there's a moon tide, the water's sound is even friendlier and
always quiet, like it's whispering, just real small baby waves,
whoosh nice and quiet whoosh quiet whoosh like you can fall
asleep in a second. And it sounds kind of weird to say but I
trust that soft sound like I trust the Water. And the Blessed
Mother. Just listening collecting my thoughts and holding
them inside for safe keeping. And no one can tell how tall
you are when you're in the water and what's great's that even
though it hides my body, it shows my face. It's like everyone's
the same size so no one even knows I'm tall and you don't

have to feel all clumsy like you do playing basketball cause the water kind of lets you be graceful, almost like a Dancer moving your legs and your arms like you're this beautiful bird fish. I can almost even <u>love</u> my tall body when it stretches across the water cause then I'm a sleek fish and the taller I am the better, I can even be a giant and still be beautiful in the water. The water takes care of everything.

Another Thing I Failed At

On earth though I feel mostly like a Scaredy Cat and a Loser and everyone can see everything you do cause your Big Stupid head's popping up over all the other kids and reaching almost to the trees. And some days you don't feel so great like when your clothes look ugly and really creepy or you're wearing something Mom says you have to or your hair doesn't dry right so it's sticking out all over or maybe you're feeling Gawky so you wish you could disappear. And people just decide you can do things <u>because</u> you're Tall. Like play basketball or softball. Just because you're closer to the net the Coach and even the Nuns say You must be a great Forward so you have to be part of the team even if you don't want to because you know they're wrong no matter what they say you know you can't play basketball. But they'll insist, Don't worry you'll learn. With your height you're a natural. You'll be great! But that's another thing I failed at, I just can't not be scared of the ball coming at me so instead of trying to catch it I turn and run away and that makes the coach yell things at me like <u>Where are you going, Joan</u>? You're supposed to be trying to <u>Get the ball, not Run Away from it</u>! and what can be funnier than an almost 6 Foot Tall Girl in a Blue Stupid Gym Suit playing basketball and <u>Running Away from the Ball</u>? The same thing happens when they make me play softball, I hate it, striking out all the time cause I get so scared when the ball starts coming that my whole body jumps back from my chest to my tush without me even deciding that I want it to. And everyone can see you every single minute doing every Stupid Thing.

Like when Mom sends you to Braren's for bread or liverwurst and you'll be praying and praying Please Blessed Mother don't let them be out let me walk up the street without seeing any of them hanging out by Ferricks or Richie Feighans waiting for me giggling and whispering as soon as they see me and I hate them there waiting in the alley for me to walk by but inside yourself you know all they're saying is true you're a Gawk You're Huge walking up the block taking up the whole middle of the street the whole complete middle your Huge Gigantic Body looking down from the sky and it just never happens that they see me and don't stop talking and start snickering and howling slapping each other and I'll be pulling myself in real small inside myself wishing I was invisible but my back real straight cause there's no way I'll let them see they hurt me even if I know they're right. And even though I might've wanted to laugh too if I saw myself walking there so Huge above everyone I wouldn't let myself even a little or smile even cause it's so mean.

A Real Giant

ow this new kid, Mike Woods moved in on our block. He's kind of nice but he makes the Giant Problems worse cause he's <u>6 feet 6 inches and he's only 13</u>! or maybe even 12. He walks around with his head down and his shoulders all slumped like he's feeling bad all the time and he probably is cause not only is he the tallest kid I ever saw but he has no parents, I think they just died or something so he came to Edgewater to live with his aunt. And he never talks to anyone and no one talks to him, they just laugh and call him dumb names like Beanstalk and Stretch and Jolly Green Giant like they call me and they think it's really a riot saying we make a good pair Two Jolly Green Giants.

I really feel sorry for Mike but I can't be too nice or friendly to him even though it's what God wants cause maybe he'll like me cause he thinks I'm the only girl he can get but I don't want him to. I wish I didn't feel that way but I can't help it, I'd be so ashamed if everyone thought I liked Mike and he was my boyfriend. And I'm sure not going to like <u>him</u> and be his girlfriend even if it is his only chance cause I have the same problem or almost. So I don't want to hang out with him and have everyone laugh at me, it's like admitting I can't get anyone else to like me except another Giant and that would be kind of admitting I'm a Total Loser. Besides

Mike's <u>really</u> scary cause it seems like his body <u>does</u> plan on being a Giant and if I hang out with him and we talk to each other, it'll happen to me. Except for his Huge Body that never stops growing, he seems like a pretty normal kind of kid so if it can happen to him, it can for sure happen to me. And Mike always looks at me with his eyes all dark and shadowy like they almost want to cry. I feel bad that I'm not nicer to him, for sure I'm not loving him as myself. What if Jesus acted like that? maybe He wouldn't want to know me cause of <u>me</u> being so tall, then I'd be totally completely alone just like I'm letting Mike be. But lucky for him he came up with a great answer to the Loneliness Cause No One Wants to Have Anything to Do With You Problem, instead of staying in regular school he's leaving at the end of the summer and going into the Seminary to become a Brother or a Priest. That's a really good decision cause he can kind of take care of his soul and be one of God's Favorites <u>and</u> not have any more problems with the kids laughing and never having any girlfriends and for sure in the Seminary kids won't be calling anybody names and they'll be acting like you're normal even when you aren't so I'm really happy for him cause it always hurts me that he hurts so much.

Kind of Confusing

he only thing that matters to God Sister says is your Soul. What God wants is for us to pretend the Body isn't there. And the body doesn't only mean Sex, what about worrying all the time about your knees hurting when you're supposed to be praying and feeling so tired you don't want to get up for Mass and all the Near Occasions? They're all problems with the Body. But Mike and I can <u>never</u> pretend that the Body's not there, the other kids won't ever let us forget it. And maybe God really <u>does</u> want me to be a Giant to make up to Jesus for the Cross He had to carry. But of course ours is <u>Nothing</u> even being a giant, compared to the one He had <u>with the hammer and the nails and having to hang there for three whole hours</u> so maybe it <u>is</u> God's will that I'm a Giant? Now my belly's burning really bad and my brain's getting all hot and black black inside I'm really sorry to be asking Dear Jesus but I was wondering if You could <u>please</u> not make me a Giant. I know it's selfish but couldn't You find something else besides me having to be any Bigger than I already am I want so much to be like everybody else and already I'm not so could You please Lord maybe decide that being This Tall is enough of a Cross I promise You I <u>am</u> suffering but maybe this much could be enough

Disgusting

ll of a sudden I'm getting Sties on my eyes. And Colitis too. That's what Dr. Green calls the burning pains I always get in my belly. The Sties get so Big you can't call them sties anymore, you have to call them Boils. And I get Boils on my toes too and under my arms and you can't even pretend they're not there cause they hurt so much they make your head hurt and your arms too and everyone can see them you're in 7th grade and Hugely Tall and you get Gigantic Boils so you can't walk around not even for one tiny second without everyone seeing something <u>else</u> about you that's disgusting like your huge Red Toe that started out as a little ingrown toenail but wouldn't stop til it became the Hugest thing you ever saw. And last Sunday one came out on my <u>eye</u>! right there on my right eye at the edge where the lashes come out. It starts out tiny but all of a sudden it gets Huge like everything else about me and it starts to almost move like the candles you light for the Souls but all of a sudden it turns into a huge fat Worm hanging off your eye starting out being your eyelid all white and skin color then pink getting redder and redder til it's maroon and there's a white point at the tip that's where the Core is, the Core's where the Poison is. That's mostly when Mom says we have to go to Dr. Green, even after days and days taking care of them ourselves by bathing them with Epsom Salts or Boric Acid, they keep getting bigger and bigger and more and more disgusting. It's so scary hearing Mom talking about what we have to do next with the Monster Boils, she always knows what the problem is before we go to Dr. Green and he always agrees with her but we still have to go to him cause Mom can't give you needles and <u>lance</u> Boils and take your tonsils out.

Anyway the last chance for us to get the boil to break is the Drawing Salve, this greasy black stuff but if that doesn't work we have to give up and get Dad to take us to Dr. Green to <u>Cut</u> it open cause it won't break itself. Every time I think of the Lancing, my head gets all woozy and fuzzy and my stomach all fluttery like a million butterflies are flying around and smashing into each other and then it's all black inside my eyes and I think that's when I almost faint. See the Core's the ball in the middle of the boil that keeps traveling and making new boils come out in other places like your other eye or under your arm or your big toe cause these boils're so big they'd never fit on the smaller toes so the Core's the Enemy and we're in Big Trouble if we don't get it out. And it's not even enough to have the stupid boil break and have all the other junk come out, if you don't get the Core, you for sure get another boil. I know this is pretty disgusting stuff to be talking about but you might not know what the big deal is about boils and why I'd even be mentioning them in the first place. Anyway, the thing about the Drawing Salve is that it's the messiest stuff in the world. Besides being extremely Ugly and Disgusting, it ruins everything, your clothes, towels, even your pillowcase. Anything it gets on, it ruins and no matter how hard Mom tries, she can't get the stains out. But that doesn't stop her. She'll wait and give the soaking and the salve a few extra days to do the trick but if that doesn't work, it's Dr. Green. But

God must have been listening cause He jumped right in and fixed it, he made Mom so good at taking care of the boils that Dr. Green <u>never</u> has to lance them even that one time when we went all the way over there to the Grand Concourse to see him, by the time he looked at it, it had already broken and the Core was out.

The Colitis started before the Boils. A few months ago maybe. When it first started, the doctor said I had a Nervous Stomach. It seemed funny that a stomach gets nervous. Later they started calling it Colitis, that means that every time I get scared or ashamed or nervous or guilty, besides the burning in my chest and feeling nauseous or the shaking, I get awful pains in my belly so I can't stand up straight and then it'll be burning too and I have to go to the bathroom all the time.

Anyway to help with the Colitis, the doctor and Mom say I'm not supposed to worry about things. But I don't know <u>how</u> to stop, I have lots of problems like the Boils and the worrying about my Soul and not being as good as God and Dad wish I was and no matter how hard I try not wanting to be a Nun and Sonny Hating me and Mom being Mad and not talking to me and being Too Tall and of course No Boyfriends and a whole bunch of other things that keep jumping up inside my brain. I even worry about school even though I get good marks all the time. I remember one time in the fourth grade when we were taking tests, Sr. Mary Consolata stopped Mom and Dad after Mass on Sunday and told them they should tell me not to worry cause I did real well in all my tests. She's another pretty Mean nun who's nice sometimes. But Sister and the Doctor and even Mom don't say <u>how</u> to stop worrying, they act like it's something you can just do if you want to and try hard enough. But Mom does try to help me. I think that's why one time when the boil broke out on my toe so I couldn't wear shoes, Mom didn't listen when the Doctor told her to cut a giant Hole in my school shoes to make room for the toe. That would've been pretty embarrassing having to walk around not only with an ingrown toenail that turned into a boil but with shoes that had a huge piece cut out of the top so you could see this stupid big Ugly Toe all wrapped up and bandaged like a really fat Turban. But Dr. Green thought that would be okay and told me not to worry about the other kids laughing cause they probably wouldn't and if they did, they aren't important anyhow if they're going to be that mean who cares about them?

But Mom must've understood how I felt because without even telling me, she had Dad drive her down to Westchester Square one night to buy me sandals, the most beautiful sandals I ever saw with yellow and blue and red and purple straps and lucky for her she didn't have to go to Footsaver, she could just buy me a pair of regular size 10s cause the sandals are open. Anyway the sandals are the one good thing about the infected toes which come either from picking my toenails which it's true I do so I have to say it even though it's Disgusting or from traveling boils. And they're a really great solution to the Kids Laughing Problem cause they'll be so busy looking at my beautiful sandals, they'll hardly even notice my big stupid bandaged toe. That's definitely one time that Mom helped me a lot with the worrying cause no matter what the doctor says, I just can't feel that the kids don't matter, I don't want them to but they do.

Just Jealous

I can't remember if I ever even tried to tell Mom any of the feelings I have inside myself, I don't think so. For sure I don't talk to her about the Tallness cause she tries so hard to tell me it's something Great, All the Models are Tall and Everyone Wants to be Tall and The Other Kids are Just Jealous. She keeps saying they really want to be just like me and they can't, that's why they laugh at me and tease me. So I don't tell her, she'd just feel bad and anyway there's just no way she'll agree with me that my height's this Huge problem. She'll just try even harder to tell me all the reasons that Being Tall is the Best Thing in the World and I'll want her to Just Stop Saying It!

But Mom just never lets any of us kids have problems, specially outside. So she makes believe we don't, whatever's wrong, she'll just make our favorite cake or buy me a new outfit and we'll feel fine. She likes things a certain way and if they aren't she'll fix them, like when she doesn't like the way the kitchen looks, she'll tear down the wallpaper and put up new stuff that makes the kitchen all bright and cheery. Or the dresser. This is the best set up yet, she'll say. Or when the kids tease me she takes me out and buys me new clothes so I'll feel pretty and the tallness will go away like she can fix me just like she fixes the kitchen. Or she'll just say No, that's not the way it is or That's not how you feel. And she thinks no one's better than we are, it's almost like she's being a little bit snobby. If we do anything wrong, she says it's because our friends are making us. Our Best Friends are our Family and we shouldn't trust Outsiders and if our friends don't treat us like we're their very best friends on earth, better than anyone Mom will almost hate them and never forgive them and she'll be mad at us for talking to them. What's weird is Mom thinks we're so great outside but not so great <u>inside</u> with her. I think she worries that we'll like our friends more than her, so she doesn't like them.

Pretty Normal

om's not the only one who says I'm lucky. Sr. Mary Lucille, my 6th grade teacher, says so too and whenever I'm around her I end up feeling Pretty Normal. I totally love her, even though she scares me a little cause she's always laughing and acting like you can still be happy being a Nun. So it's pretty amazingly cool for me that Sr. Mary Lucille says she has terrible handwriting and I'm so lucky cause mine's so great. And what's totally completely Amazing is that one day last year she called me up to the blackboard and said that I was going to teach Penmanship to the class, just like that. After that every Friday afternoon during Penmanship period, she called for me and I stood at the board teaching the class and she sat in the back like I always do cause no one can see over me. The first time she sat in my seat I couldn't believe it, I never saw a nun sitting in a kid's seat. There she was just like all the other kids, copying everything I wrote on the board like it was important and it wasn't even a joke and she wasn't pretending. Even now that I'm in 7th grade she still calls for me to come down and teach Penmanship to her class. It's totally great. I love being the Teacher. So I guess she's right, I really am lucky.

Easter Outfit

omorrow's Easter. Easter's a really happy day and an extremely important day for God and Catholics. It's the day Jesus proved <u>for sure</u> He was God. No way He could be dead one minute, then Rise, push that huge rock aside then walk around talking to people and even healing them if He wasn't God. Sister even says that Easter's more important than Christmas. That seems pretty confusing though cause I don't know how any of this could have happened without Him being born first but that's what she says so that's it. Anyway besides having colored eggs and Easter baskets, you're lucky cause you're going to High Mass which means there're three priests <u>singing</u> the Mass and it lasts an hour and a half or <u>two hours</u> even but of course you'd never complain about your knees hurting and your nylons ripping from all the kneeling cause this is the Lord's Big Day. You get beautiful new clothes and wear them to Mass like this is a huge Party that the priests're having for God and everyone has to get dressed up in fancier clothes than usual. That's so great. My outfit this year's Gorgeous, a puffy blue taffeta dress and a white coat with big sleeves and a bouncy straw color hat with about a million skinny skinny every color ribbons trailing down my back. And of course Nylons. I love my Nylons but I only get one pair for Easter and no matter how hard I try, I end up with Monster Runs in them. And what's really bad is that it's always in the morning at Church after we've been kneeling so long on those scratchy wooden kneelers with no red puffy cushions like they have in some richer churches like St. Benedict's so I get Huge Holes in my nylons. One stupid splinter starts the whole mess and it just gets worse and worse and I hate it that everyone can see them when I walk around Edgewater with my friends after Easter dinner showing off my clothes.

5 Feet 11 1/2 Inches

I even wore <u>Heels</u> to Church for Easter and not those low pygmy ones that look like someone sawed them off in the middle. I try to convince Catherine that wearing flats or those stupid cut-off pretend heels when you're dressed up is like admitting you're embarrassed about being tall and like saying you don't want to be. But I <u>am</u> and I <u>don't</u> want to be, she'll say. And she's only 5 feet 8 1/2! So Catherine and I are really different about the Tallness, she doesn't care if people know she doesn't like it. Not me, I mean I'm <u>5 feet 11 and 1/2 inches</u> so even if I wear flats or low pigmy heels from now til Doomsday, there's no way I'll look normal size so why look even more ugly by twisting my body in weird stupid shapes that don't even work so the boys can laugh even more. No way they'll think I'm not proud of my height, I think even Catherine thinks I'm proud. I never even told <u>her</u> I almost Hate what I look like. Nobody knows. And that's the way you want it to be, keeping your secrets inside and not telling them to anybody even your Best Friend or your Sister. Only your notebook. And of course you have to admit to your Mom or Dad or Sister even that you did something if they ask. And Confession where you tell Father everything, that's the only other time you <u>have to</u> talk about what's inside of you. The bad stuff you did I mean, Father doesn't really care about Tallness, he'd just say God created you the way He wanted you to be so you should be <u>proud</u> and <u>grateful</u> and you know that's something you could never be even if you tried forever.

But you never have to tell anybody about always being afraid you're a Giant and wishing you could maybe Make Out someday which it's true, I do and how much you love the Beach and how you're kind of embarrassed being Irish. And you certainly can't go around telling everybody on the block maybe that you wet your bed and sometimes your Mom seems kind of mean. But still sometimes you wish you could feel better like you do after Confession and you know how great you feel like you're all clean again and not hating yourself for doing something so awful cause you just have to say your Penance and that sin and the bad feelings go away. And you can be happy again and not feeling like maybe Jesus isn't loving you as much any more. You know how nice it feels having someone to talk to about sins so how great it would be to talk to someone about things that aren't sins but still hurt you alot. But you can't cause everybody would think you were Dumb or a Jerk or a Dirty Pig maybe or a Gawk or you would be committing a crime almost against the family. Never tell anyone what goes on inside our four walls Mom always says. But lucky for me at least I can write it so I don't have to feel completely Lonely having a million sad things going on inside me.

Phony

ike one secret I have is sometimes I'm holy <u>on purpose</u>. Like I'll be dishing out the supper and I'll give myself less than anyone else just like Mom does and I'll be feeling all good inside when Daddy says I'm so Good and Unselfish. But when I think about that now I feel like I'm pretending and Faking and beating out the others by being Phony and its Burning inside my belly again and in my chest and throat and its filling up my whole insides so its hard to hold my head up cause it wants to fall down Dead on my chest I wish I could be <u>really</u> Good Really Really Good like Dad. But no one can be as good as Dad.

Another thing I'm totally Ashamed of but it's True so I have to say it is about my night prayers. See when I get into bed I fold my hands on my chest, fingers and palms touching and pointing up to Heaven like a church, I say my prayers that way even though I know I should say them kneeling by the bed. I feel guilty for being so Lazy so most nights I get out of bed and get down on my knees. But that's not really the embarrassing part, I'm talking about the Hands Folded While I'm Praying Part. Mom and Dad always look in on us to see if we're sleeping and covered with blankets and I love hearing Mom say Look at her, she fell asleep saying her prayers and Dad saying She's such a good girl. That's why I'm so Ashamed, I was wide awake with my eyes closed and I folded my hands <u>on purpose</u> when I heard them coming in the door. I folded them just <u>so they'd see me and think I was Good</u> and say Look at her, she fell asleep saying her prayers! And Sonny knows too, one morning when Mom mentioned me falling asleep praying, he leaned over and whispered, You weren't asleep. You just went to bed you <u>Phony</u>! And I hate being called a Phony, especially by Sonny. I totally Hate it but it's true, this time Sonny was right.

Dad's Sad and Mad

Being a Phony's like Lying and Daddy'd really be Ashamed and even Mad if he found out I was one. Mostly he never gets mad except one or two times and that was Awful. So I do everything I can not to <u>ever</u> make him look at me in that really Scary way where he starts to look like an almost Monster, but sometimes when I'm really failing at Controlling the Bad Thoughts, I'll picture his face with his lip pushing out and out getting fatter and fatter til all of a sudden its not his mouth anymore it's a <u>Beak</u> almost and it's saying in a mean scary voice You're <u>Disgusting</u>! and He can't stand to even look at you You should be <u>Ashamed</u> of yourself! So every time a bad thought jumps up inside my head my belly starts burning and I'll be thinking How Weak I Am What a Big Disappointment to the Lord and Dad. All I want is for Dad to be smiling and happy with me and proud that I'm his good Catholic girl who loves the Lord with her whole heart and her whole soul so why is my brain always filling up with Bad Thoughts of not wanting to be a nun or not wanting to say the Rosary or complaining about my knees hurting or my nylons running or even for an almost second wondering what condemned movies show, all sorts of Bad Awful Thoughts that hurt God. And being a Phony. And you feel like somehow Dad knows what's going on inside your brain and you know he's very very Sad like God is in that picture of the Sacred Heart with the heart bleeding and the eyes really really sad.

The Rosary

I even have problems with the Rosary. I mean concentrating completely and perfectly and not having any thoughts about how I wish I didn't have to say it or about my homework or being scared of the way Sonny's looking at me. See every night after supper we all kneel for the Rosary. It's always Dad who picks the leader. The only time the order changes is when one of us brings home the Statue. The Statue is the Blessed Virgin dressed in the clothes she wore when she appeared to Bernadette, the blue gown with the white veil and her hair real long and blonde and kind of straight and parted in the middle and her arms out like she's pleading or saying Why? Or maybe it was the three children of Fatima. Anyway each class at St. Frances has its own Statue and it's a special honor for a kid to be able to take the Statue home in her little coffin, the kind I figure they bury very tiny babies in. Everyone in the class gets their turn bringing the statue home for a whole week. And the reason it comes home is so God and the nuns and the Blessed Mother will be sure that the whole family kneels together and says The Family Rosary out loud. Just then I almost thought that maybe the kids who only have to say it when they bring the Statue and not every night like we have to in our house are lucky. That's the stuff that always sneaks in and keeps hurting Jesus. Everyone kneeling in front of the Statue with the kid who brought it home as the Leader is the way it's supposed to be.

Anyway, we just turn our chairs around and kneel right there in the Dining Room with all of us on our knees against our chairs with our backsides to the table. We're supposed to just have the chair there for an emergency in case we get weak or have to lean for a few minutes. Otherwise we're supposed to be kneeling with our backs and heads straight like Dad's are. Most of the time though we lean on the seat of the chair through the whole Rosary. Sometimes though if you're sick you're allowed to sit. Mom's lucky a lot and says she has to sit cause she's having one of her weak spells and Dad can't say anything about that, she's a grown-up too but that never means you can skip it completely. You're never so sick that you can't say it at least from your bed. For those special occasions when someone's too sick to get out of bed, we bring our chairs in or kneel at the side of their bed. But what's the big deal about having to kneel for 15 or 20 minutes which mostly becomes 25 or 30 cause Dad always wants to finish the Rosary with one of those long litanies to the Blessed Mother where he says all the names she's known as like Queen of Peace, Queen of Heaven and Earth and Our Lady of Fatima. There are maybe 50 or 100 of them because she's very good and in charge of a lot. After each one, we say Pray for Us. But who cares if you have to kneel for 30 minutes or even 45? It's a chance for a nice little sacrifice, which sad to say you've been forgetting about lately.

Anyway, the leader's like the Boss that night. They start off the praying with The Apostles' Creed and then one Our Father, three Hail Marys and One Glory Be to the Father and then The Five Joyful Mysteries of the Rosary or the

Five Sorrowful Mysteries or the Five Glorious, each day's different. And I don't know why they're Mysteries except maybe they're things you aren't supposed to understand because they're too complicated for humans. Only God and the Saints and the Nuns maybe understand the Mysteries. Anyway the next thing the leader says is The First Joyful Mystery, The Annunciation, if it's a Joyful day and then they'll lead us in the Our Father and ten Hail Marys and one Glory Be. All those make one decade and each mystery gets a decade. The leader says the first part of each prayer and the rest of us say the second. And we do that for all the five mysteries. Then when the Rosary's finished, the leader says the Litany naming all the names of the Blessed Virgin or zillions of Saints and the rest of us say Pray for us. So if they're all listening and according to Dad and the Nuns they always are, we have a lot of people praying for us that night.

But the problem is my knees get all hot and red and burning from pressing on the linoleum for so long and they hurt in the living room too even though we have Carpeting. We say the Rosary in the living room only when Mom's sick so she has to lie on the couch. Of course I don't say anything about the kneeling hurting to Dad and I'm sure I don't really hate it but just wish I didn't have to do it so you might say I almost hate it. I know for sure though I'm happy when I'm sick. We all are and I'll bet everybody except of course Dad gets a little bit mad at the one who's sick cause they get away without kneeling and we want that to be us. And it feels like it's never going to end. I'm ashamed to say that. This is one of the things I try so hard not to think cause it's so ungrateful to God and even mean. But I must not be trying hard enough. If I was trying <u>really really</u> hard to <u>concentrate</u> on the prayers and the Mysteries there'd be <u>no</u> room for the bad thoughts to slip in.

Sometimes I wonder if Catherine or Sonny or even Jerry wish Dad would forget about the Rosary or just not say the Litany or they could maybe be sick so they didn't have to kneel. Or if they have any of the other Not So Holy Thoughts I'm always having. But I don't think so, I mean whenever I look and I try really hard not to but sometimes my eyes just want to they always seem like they have their heads down and they're praying perfectly without one thought of wishing they didn't have to. And of course I'd never ask them cause of us never talking about what's going on inside our brain.

My Jesus

here's no point praying Daddy always says if you're wishing, even in some teeny place inside yourself that you didn't have to or you can't wait for it to be over. That used to really scare me cause it means that even if I do kneel straight for the Rosary or I go to Mass, I already spoiled it for Jesus. Maybe He's disappointed with your sacrifice and doesn't even see it as a gift at all, He doesn't want it if you aren't totally and completely <u>thrilled</u> to give it. But I've been thinking a lot about Jesus and I don't think Dad's right this time. That's not the way My Jesus would act. My Jesus <u>never</u> says you have to be Perfect, look at Mary Magdalene, she for sure wasn't perfect and it was Chastity and that's a worse sin for a girl, still Jesus loved her prayers. He loves you no matter how bad you are, like a really nice Mom or Dad. Our Lord wouldn't be mad at you I don't think, He'd just be Loving you.

A Boss

Something so cool happened about Mom and being smart and me finding out she is. See last year when Catherine started Preston High School Mom said it was time to get a job so she could start putting money away. She wants to save enough so all four of us can go to college. After paying all the bills like insurance and food and coal and Dr. Green and clothes and tuition for St. Frances <u>and</u> Preston she doesn't have any money left from Dad's paycheck so she has to earn some herself.

So now Mom works for Catholic Charities as a Case Worker. I'm not sure what that is but it sounds pretty important and I know Mom goes every day to take care of people who're sick or in trouble like old Mrs. Goodkind who lives alone all the way down on Catherine Slip Street and who reads love stories. Mom says that the first day she got to her house, Mrs. Goodkind showed her her box of Romance books under the bed. Mrs. Goodkind's what Mom calls a Long-Term Case. Mom's boss Sr. Maria says Mom's her Best Worker so she always calls on her in really tough cases. Mom's regular job is to go to a house and see a woman who just had a baby or is sick maybe and there's no one to help her and maybe even no heat and no food like that Spanish lady over in the Morrisania Section who calls Mom Santa Maria. Mom's a nurse and a cook and a Mom for the new babies or for the other kids in the house. And she has to do the shopping and make the beds and I know for a fact she has to empty old Mr. Fisher's bedpan and give him a bath! But does she have to wash <u>down there</u>? Of course she doesn't tell me and I wouldn't ask but I <u>do</u> wonder a lot and I feel really sorry for her that she has to see people's bodies especially men's and give them baths.

Anyway once Mom gets her Program going, Sr. Maria will send some other case worker in to follow Mom's plan. And Mom goes some place else to see what they need or if they're only faking, and whatever Mom says goes. But sometimes people like Mrs. Goodkind don't want another case worker, they only want Mom and they plead with Sr. Maria to send Mom and if she doesn't they'll call Mom at home and beg her to come back. That means that sometimes Mom <u>is</u> sent back especially if things get worse like when Mrs. Goodkind fell and broke her hip and refused to let anyone but Mom in the door. So Sr. Maria had to give in, she called Mom at 6 o'clock that morning and told her to go to Mrs. Goodkind.

And I don't know why but sick people only get taken care of during the week. I guess Mom worries about that too cause she always pops in on Mrs. Goodkind Saturday afternoon or Sunday after dinner when she and Dad go for a ride in Gorgeous George. That's really great cause then Mrs. Goodkind doesn't have to be so lonely living all by herself all the way downtown.

After School Jobs

I am the Mother when Mother is out, Catherine always says. Change your school clothes and Hang up your uniform and No more toast, you won't finish your dinner. See ever since Mom went to work Catherine's the Boss over us. She cleans too and I cook, I make supper everyday except Saturday and Sunday. The one problem I have is that even though I always ask Dad to buy spices like garlic and pepper and stuff, most of the time Mom tells him not to. So I'm pretty happy when she says okay. She thinks the food will taste bad if you add too much to it or maybe Dad'll get heartburn but he never does. I wish I could try some new things but Mom says let's keep to our regular schedule like Monday chicken with rice, Tuesday hamburger or calves liver, Wednesday sausages, Thursday ham or <u>Tongue!</u> and Fridays always fish like flounder or fish sticks or tuna with noodles. And of course we always have potatoes, mostly mashed with lots of butter and milk and onion too and maybe string beans or broccoli or carrots or corn with lots of butter melting on top making little puddles in the dish. Sometimes Mom will let me make spaghetti with tomato sauce when I make the hamburgers. Or macaroni and cheese, that's my favorite besides tapioca pudding with raisins and of course chocolate pudding. And Mom even trusts me with the Pressure Cooker even when she's not home and if you're not totally and completely careful you could cause a huge explosion that would burn the whole house down and kill everybody. But Mom showed me how to use it and even though I get a little scared sometimes when the steam starts to fly out I still use it.

Only Mom

Before she started working Mom hardly ever went out until that one winter when our cousin Lilly got sick, she was Pregnant and the doctor said she'd lose the baby if she got out of bed. Mom says that a woman of forty-one having a baby is dangerous so Mom and Dad Loving Thy Neighbor as Thyself went up to Mount Vernon <u>every night</u> after supper and the Rosary for a whole six months so Mom could take care of Lilly while Dad helped her husband, his cousin Hugh take care of their Bar and Grill, the Dublin House. I'm pretty proud of Mom cause she's the one who had to give the baths and then clean up the house and Lilly isn't even <u>her</u> cousin. But because of Mom Lilly's baby was born and Lilly's feeling better and the whole family's great again.

Mom's even nice to Mr. Shaw who nobody else likes and that seems pretty amazing since she has lots of problems liking people and here she is liking someone no one else likes. Every-time one of us starts complaining that he's just a Crank and a Crab yelling at the kids all the time and being a Cheap Skate not fixing up the beach Mom says he's not so bad. I think that's because he lets her be late with the rent when she can't pay it on time. Anyway Mr. Shaw owns the beach but Blackie Decker had to start the Edgewater Park Beach Association so we could fix it up ourselves, the Dads I mean. All we want is for him to send his truck with strong guys driving them. But he won't. First there's the problem of the horseshoe crabs that you have to get rid of cause millions of them are always washing in with the tide and it's hard to walk and they're pretty smelly too and the cement around the bulkhead's cracked and needs Reinforcement, Blackie says. Then of course The Association voted for some pretty amazing things like rafts and diving boards and sliding ponds and lights that stay on ·til ten o'clock so we can go night swimming. And Blackie and the Dads are doing all the work and all the families are paying their dues for the rafts and the slides, everyone's working their heads off trying to make something special for the kids, Loving Thy Neighbor As Thyself which I don't think Grumpy Old Mr. Shaw does. So he's pretty lucky that Mom likes him, so he isn't completely Alone with not one single person in the world even liking him.

Like I Fit

I can't stop thinking about Catherine though, having so many problems with Mom. How can Mom like creepy Mr. Shaw and not like her <u>own</u> daughter? I wish Catherine had a private place to go to like I do. Like the Water. I like to picture diving into it and letting it take me wherever it wants, even miles away. Like I belong to it. I can swim along in the undertow and the water will carry me with it to the edge of some new shore. Or maybe I can live inside it forever, I like that thought, swimming forever in the water's nice warm belly. But I hope I can keep my human body, when we're underwater and size makes no difference, the longer a body is the more graceful it is and Beautiful.

†
JMJ

Kind of Pretty

ow that the boils are gone, I'm not so scared to look in the mirror. And every once in a while besides all the old ladies and Mom saying it, I'll look at myself real fast when I'm passing a mirror or a car window and I'll catch my face looking kind of nice. Still a little too round like a moon face and my eyes a little too squinty and too much teeth when I smile. Lots of times though I don't even care like when I'm bursting out laughing, then the teeth probably show but so what? I love laughing. And I've always liked my long and thick brown hair, you could almost say it's Dark Red like Auburn, that's much more Glamorous. The same with my eyes, some people call them Hazel, that's okay but not great. Hazel's kind of blue and grey and green and I'm not so crazy about eyes that can't decide what color they want to be so I like to call mine green, green eyes are very Sophisticated. Liking the way you look is liking the way God made you and that's like giving Him a compliment. The only thing He worries about with the body is that you might make it too important and forget that it's His Temple, the body's only there to carry the Soul and I for sure would never forget about that.

JMJ

My Uniform

On school days though, most of the time you don't like what you look like cause you have to wear Uniforms. From first grade til you're seniors in high school. Twelve years of wearing the same old Ugly clothes, one for the eight years in grammar school and another one that's completely ugly too for four years in high school. So no one gets to see how pretty your new blouse is and how you have a poodle skirt too and a cinch belt plus a million other things you're dying to wear. Everybody in the whole school looks totally completely the same whether they're fat or tall or skinny or short, everyday the same old Boring clothes. It's true that I do wish I looked like everybody else but I'm only wishing that about the Tallness. And even when it's brand new with no ink marks on the skirt or chalk or messed up pleats, our uniform's ugly. And your shoes are too even when they're not scuffed and flopping all around cause they're too wide cause school shoes don't come in quadruple A. We wear navy blue Jumpers with no sleeves. The blouse is always white til it becomes Tattletale Grey from the stupid blouses having to be washed maybe a thousand times cause you keep them forever.

Lucky for us though Sister lets us wear our own clothes for our Birthday. But it's only one measly day. That's why you're always dying for your Mom to let you take your uniform to the dry cleaners cause then you won't have it for a week maybe and you'll have to be wearing regular clothes every day. And everybody in the whole class will be looking at you and thinking how lucky you are to have so many great outfits that you have enough to wear something different for every day. Like your turquoise poodle skirt. And you'll feel extra Happy walking around school like you look maybe kind of great and you're even happy to be going to school.

Aunts

It's Sunday so that means it's Aunt Eileen's turn to come over. Lucky for us we have three Aunts, two totally great and our Favorites, Aunt Eileen and Aunt May who I told you about and one really nice but not so great, Aunt Rose who's my Godmother too which is sort of too bad but so what if my Godmother isn't totally Great. And they're all Irish but Aunt May talks like a regular American person, not one who came from the Old Country. And she's very very smart even if it's true that she <u>is</u> a little bit fat. But so what, who cares about fat?

And we're crazy about Aunt Eileen too. Even if she <u>does</u> talk with a Brogue. She's Mom's younger sister and she's kind of Glamorous in a working lady way and she wears suits, with white or baby blue blouses with Peter Pan collars and her hair in a Page Boy and she's very Pretty. And she Smokes Cigarettes! And you like your friends to know you have such a glamorous Aunt even if she does come from the Old Country. I think when I get older I might want to be like Aunt Eileen, she's Sonny's Godmother but she loves all of us. One Easter she came for dinner with her girlfriend Hannah. We were really little, me and my friend Ginny like maybe in the second grade or the third and I asked her if I could try on her Easter hat, then the jacket to her suit. And she ended up taking off her whole Easter Outfit even her high heels and maybe even her nylons and putting on one of Mom's housedresses and I ended up wearing the whole outfit like it was really mine, for as long as I wanted, even outside too. And she got her girlfriend to do the same thing so Ginny could have a lady's outfit too.

And for your birthday it's so cool cause Aunt Eileen'll <u>ask</u> you what you want instead of just deciding for herself. When I was maybe 6, she asked me if I wanted her to take me to the Rodeo or would I like my own umbrella or a brand new crispy $5 bill. I don't remember, but I think I chose the Rodeo cause it's so much more exciting than an umbrella even though no girl around has a yellow one or a red that's only theirs so that'd be cool too and $5 is for sure cool. Still the Rodeo's nothing I've ever seen before except in movies with Roy Rogers or Gene Autry maybe and Dale Evans. I wish I could remember but maybe I don't cause I didn't go. I love remembering, it makes the great thing happen over and over.

Anyway, no way is Aunt Rose as great as Aunt Eileen. Aunt Rose isn't pretty and she isn't glamorous and it's embarrassing to say but she isn't too smart. Aunt Rose isn't like a regular lady or even a Mom cause she really likes beer. When she babysits for us, we'll ask her if she wants a glass of beer and she'll say yes and pretty soon she'll start getting sleepy. That's what's always so great cause she'll have a nice little nap and then we can do anything we want, like Sonny and Jerry jumping on the couch or piano or Catherine inviting Frances Freitag and John Ferrick over. I usually don't do too much cause I'm always Scared of God seeing me. Or Mom asking what I did and me not being able to lie and getting in Big Trouble. But it's kind of fun watching the others go crazy. Having Aunt Rose watching us is like having no one watching us. And that's mostly great but it's kind of embarrassing too, who ever heard of an aunt who's also a Mom who the kids can fool and trick and she doesn't even know it? Even if you think Moms can't read or spell coming from The Old Country and the farm like I used to worry about with Mom, Moms always catch you and know what you're doing even if you just did it and they weren't even home! They know even if you're just <u>thinking</u> about doing it. But not Aunt Rose and that's maybe good for fooling around but mostly bad for wanting an Aunt who's smart.

And the other thing that's kind of weird about Aunt Rose is she isn't smart about cooking either. Once Mom was in the hospital and Aunt Rose had to take care of us and make Thanksgiving dinner and she made Corned Beef Hash instead of Turkey! Like she didn't even know there was anything wrong with that. We were all so upset and crying almost but of course we never let her know. And we wouldn't tell Dad either cause she's his sister, he might be mad that we weren't being grateful and caring about the wrong things like stupid turkeys instead of people. But still we never in a million years had anything but Turkey and Stuffing and Mashed Potatoes and Turnips and Creamed Onions and Mom's Apple Pie and Pumpkin and of course Cranberry Sauce and Cider. We were so unhappy I couldn't imagine any Sadder thing than a family with a Mom in the hospital and an Aunt who makes Corned Beef Hash <u>with Fried Eggs on Top</u>! for Thanksgiving Dinner. It's just that she didn't know that what she was doing made no sense.

That was so Mean saying that stuff about Poor Aunt Rose who's so completely nice and loves me so much and here I am saying she's not smart and a failure as a babysitter and too bad she's my Godmother. It would make her so sad if she knew

I said that. Completely Totally Sad with her heart Smashed in. For sure it would hurt Daddy and I know it hurts you too Dear Jesus that I'm not charitable at all and Loving My Neighbor as Myself. I <u>try</u> to like Aunt Rose as much as Aunt May and Aunt Eileen but I just can't.

Mom's Heart

nyway even though Mom isn't too crazy about girl-friends, I think she really likes it that she and Dad have sisters. See last time she was over, I heard Aunt Eileen saying that not only did their Mom Die but she Died when Mom was only 6 years old! Their little brother Dan was being born and their Mom was <u>Dying!</u> in her own bed. Mom stayed by the bedroom door the whole time so she saw her Mom's face all twisted and breaking from hurting so much and all of a sudden she's dead. And her body stayed there in the bed til the ladies came and washed her and dressed her and got her ready for the Funeral and lots of people came to say they were sorry. But after that nobody talked about her Mom anymore, Aunt Eileen says it was almost like she never even lived, like they never even <u>had</u> a Mom. And after her Mom Died, Dan became Mom's Favorite. So he kind of helped her with the Loneliness Problem cause even though their Dad was around, he was always working real hard running the farm and cook-ing and washing and stuff. The kids pitched in and Mom did too by taking care of Baby Dan like he was really her own little Baby.

I feel so bad thinking about poor Mom being a little girl and having her Mom die when her brother's being born. I never heard anything so Sad all Mom's life with no Mom. I don't think I'd ever stop crying and my heart would be always breaking if anything happened to my Mom, I don't think I'd want to live anymore if Mom died. And I'd feel so bad about leaving Dad and Catherine and Jerry and not loving Jesus more than Mom, so I wanted to stay around til He decided I should die but still no matter how hard I try I can't make myself want to live if Mom has to die. And I don't know what to do about loving Mom more than even Jesus.

But her Mom dying wasn't the end of Mom's Problems. Aunt Eileen says Uncle Dan <u>ran away</u> when he was twelve or eleven or something and nobody ever saw him again, even Mom who was his Almost Mother. Dan always felt like it was his fault their Mom died, Aunt Eileen said and even though they all loved him a lot he always thought inside their hearts they really hated him. So Mom's heart got broken again Completely and Totally Broken <u>Two Times</u>. I don't know how she can ever even laugh or want to buy Christmas presents or make Thanksgiving dinner or go for a ride in Gorgeous George with Dad or to Hearns Basement to buy new tea cups or teach Sonny to draw, why isn't she crying every second? Losing her Mom when she's a tiny little girl and then her little brother. And since this happened to Mom her whole life was Totally Completely Ruined and inside her heart she's always hurting. That makes me want to put my arms around her and tell her I love her a whole lot, except we don't do a whole huge amount of hugging and kissing in our family but I wish God would find Uncle Dan for her. Maybe that's why she always acts so mad cause she's scared we want to run away from her too.

Another Irish Dad

oday's St. Patrick's Day, an extremely important day for Catholics and Irish people and for marching with the band down on Fifth Avenue for the Cardinal and the Mayor and maybe the President and a million other people, everybody in front of the Cathedral watching you marching for St. Patrick. It was so great, everything all green and smily and lots of Irish music that's starting to sound pretty pretty great. And when we got home, Mr. O'Shea came over with some green beer for Dad. Mr. O'Shea came from Ireland too and he's totally great. He's a retired fireman who loves kids specially Jerry and Sonny. And even me and Catherine but especially the boys. His wife's kind of crabby but when she goes to work, he'll call all the kids in the house and give us all milk and cake and cookies and fruit. Mrs. O'Shea hides all the good stuff though like fresh grapes and maybe peach ice cream and one time millions of chocolates in a big red box shaped like a heart from Valentine's Day probably and strawberries too that she's keeping for herself. But Mr. O'Shea always finds it all and gives it to us anyway. That makes her mad when she comes home from work and she'll yell a lot and tell us all it's time to go home, so we try to get out before she gets there.

Mr. O'Shea loves the way Jerry sings and Sonny draws,

he lets Sonny come down and draw anything he wants and even tells him he can borrow things like statues and hats and canes and all kinds of knick knacks if he wants to take them home to work on a painting. His son Michael is always there too, he's very handsome and nice and thinks it's great that his Dad helps all us kids. Michael's a Soldier who came home early from The War. And he's always reading cause he can't work, I don't know what happened but they must have shot him cause he's always limping and walking with a cane. And not only does Mr. O'Shea let Sonny paint in the house but he wants to <u>buy</u> Sonny's paintings too. He'll say he wants Sonny to paint him something and he always wants to give him money for it even though Sonny says No thank you. Mom and Dad never let us take money from neighbors, it isn't polite and it isn't charitable. Even Jerry has to say No thank you when Mr. O'Shea or Mr. Schadel want to give him ice cream money for singing. But even though Jerry always says No my Mom won't let me take it, he still puts his hand out so if Mr. O'Shea or Mr. Schadel <u>insist</u> on giving it to him anyway, he won't be able to help it. He makes it a little easier for them so they don't have to grab his hand and force it open.

But best of all Mr. O'Shea gave us our <u>Canoe</u>! It's true, we have the best canoe in the whole world and the totally best thing that any kid in Edgewater can get is a Boat. It used to be Michael's but he can't use it anymore so Mr. O'Shea thought it would be good for us to have. And even though it's not a speed boat, still a canoe is pretty great and we're totally crazy about it. All four of us painted it together with some leftover green paint Dad had from painting the cellar floor. And even though there's a few spots of dry rot on the side, if you're careful which we for sure are, there won't be any problem. All four of us take turns using it. We made up the rule that one of us always has to be with the canoe and if friends want to borrow it, we have to go along, we would <u>die</u> if anything happened to our canoe, we love it so much.

The Bishop

It's funny but I think I'm getting a little like Mom and Dad about being Irish. See even though Mom and Dad are really different about hitting and yelling and praying, they sure are the same about being Irish. I mean they like Mr. O'Shea and they like to eat soda bread and tea and lots of potatoes. Even I do. But they love Irish Music too. Which is really too bad for me cause I'm embarrassed about most of the stuff Mom and Dad play on the Victrola. But all of a sudden I'm even liking some Irish songs and not just the stuff we played in the parade. Like I love Danny Boy and Kevin Barry too which is kind of a war song about a poor guy who was fighting for Ireland and got hung. And I'll Take You Home Again Kathleen, there's just no song in the world that's prettier than that. It's a song about a dream I always have of being a Bride lying in the Prince's arms and he's carrying you to this special place that's your home that you love with all your heart. He's taking you in his arms so you don't have another thing to worry about. And I really hope that if I ever stop growing and the boys start growing very very fast that someday one will be strong enough to be my Prince and he'll lift me in his arms and swing me around like they do in those Fred Astaire movies.

So anyway, all of a sudden I'm almost liking being Irish.

Like I love St. Patrick's Day when everyone wears green ties and shamrocks and there are millions of leprechauns in the store windows and the men drink green beer and I'm in the Band marching in the big parade on Fifth Avenue past St. Patrick's Cathedral and the Cardinal and Mom makes Irish Soda Bread with all the raisins and lots of butter smeared all over it.

And for sure I love Dad's friend, The Bishop. He's Irish too. It's so cool that Dad who's just a regular person can be such good friends with a Bishop. And he comes right into our house and takes off his jacket and his collar with the tiny tiny purple ribbon at the top and he just kicks his shoes off and walks around in his socks laughing with Dad and telling stories about the Old Country and asking us about school and swimming and never once asking about praying. Same with Aunt May, even though she's a Nun she's never talking about praying when she's at our house. She and the Bishop're just happy and laughing and thinking Mom's cooking's great and having some more roasted potatoes and maybe an extra piece of peach upside down cake. But we don't get to see the Bishop very much, he lives all the way over in Africa taking care of all the poor Natives and trying to convert them to Catholic. I get so scared for him being a Missionary with Natives like maybe they'll throw a spear at him and kill him. I guess that would make him a Martyr which even though it's sad that he has to die for sure he'd be another of God's Favorites and knowing someone who's a Martyr could be really cool. But not for even the tiniest second would my heart not be totally broken if The Bishop had to be tortured and killed, I'm just saying if he has to be one I'll sure be proud of him.

And he never even seems scared. He acts like Natives are regular people, which I think is pretty great being so charitable cause I don't really think Natives are <u>supposed</u> to be regular people, I think they're more like in between people and animals or maybe another kind of creature that God created that's different from people or animals. And of course they don't speak English. And Natives dress kind of weird with Feathers and Rings in their noses and the ladies without blouses walking around naked even in front of the kids and they scream and jump around a lot. But the Bishop thinks that's perfectly okay and it isn't even a sin and anything they do is just fine with him. Even with no clothes on. I like that, being able to be so far from home with everything so different and still feeling like it's Normal.

†
JMJ

Far Off Places

hen I was really little I thought the other side of the water like where City Island is was The Other Side that Mom and Dad talk about. I'm really proud of them, they left home and their Moms and Dads and brothers and sisters and came to a new country where they knew no one except maybe for Mom's cousin in Rochester who had a Rooming House where too bad for her Mom worked as a maid. But Mom didn't mind being a maid, she was so deliriously happy that she could live someplace and with someone even her cousin. Of course I think it's exciting that Mom and Dad crossed the ocean to a new country but it's mostly Scary, I don't think I'd ever be able to do that. But I hope I can, I want to travel to far off places on planes and boats and see what life's like across the Ocean.

And even though I'm still not completely crazy about Ireland which mustn't be exciting at all, I mean why else would Mom and Dad and the other Greenhorns leave there, I still want to go and meet my Grandma and Grandpa before they all of a sudden die. Then off I'd go to London that has about a million buildings and Big Ben and the guys who make the laws who all wear wigs! that're kind of long and have really tight tight curls that look like rows of ropes across the back of their heads. And there's the huge Palace with the Queen and if you wait outside you can maybe see her. And I'll go to Paris too where all the love stories happen and walk around and maybe I'll meet a Prince and see the Eiffel Tower that looks like a Huge Erector Set and I'll go for boatrides on the river. And I think I'll go to Spain where they have the Bullfights which're really sad for the bulls so maybe I won't go and Italy too where they have great spaghetti and pizza and the Leaning Tower and of course the Vatican where Pope Pius lives and I'll maybe someday even see Him. And I want my own car as soon as I can get it, which won't be til after college and teaching for a while and saving up all my money so I can buy maybe a White Cadillac Convertible or a Thunderbird. But for sure I want a convertible, my hair flying and dancing all around in the wind, I love the Wind.

†
JMJ

A Slob Like Me

nd I love books, specially about Doctors taking care of sick people. I might even want to be one, maybe I'll find a Cure for some awful disease like Polio which is killing all the kids or making them crippled and just from swimming. What I'd never be though is a nurse cleaning the bedpans and being the doctor's helper instead of the one deciding things and has people helping <u>her</u>.

Anyway, my favorite thing is to get under the covers with a book and a flashlight and read, after everyone else goes to sleep so it's real quiet, totally and completely quiet. My dream is to write something big like Gone with the Wind and I think maybe I even can cause I read about Margaret Mitchell having chapters of the book all over the house, millions of yellow sheets of paper in closets, under the bed, in paper bags and not in the right order either and coffee stains all over the writing and maybe orange juice. So that means you don't have to be Neat and Perfect to be Great and Famous either. And I really want to be, even though it's not so good for a Catholic to be wanting that. But not for doing nothing, for writing big fat books with maybe a million pages that everyone wants to read and they'll maybe want to make a movie out of. That would be so glamorous, the stars in Hollywood wanting to make a movie out of something you wrote. And I

JMJ

never even <u>thought</u> about a lady being a Famous Writer but if Margaret Mitchell who's a Lady <u>and</u> a Slob can do it then maybe I can too.

Almost Normal

I can't wait for summer. My favorite sound in the whole world is waking up on Saturday morning in the beginning of June when all you can hear is the sound of outboards on the water. You know then for sure it's summer and school's almost over and there'll be nothing but your bathing suit and no shoes and no stupid uniform and lots of sun and the tar all shining and hot and bubbling and Mom making elbow macaroni with ketchup and cold hard boiled eggs for lunch and maybe even cookies. And salt from the water all over my arms and face and even my legs like white powder but rougher.

And I like not being scared, you can take me out and drop me in the middle of the Sound in a hundred feet of water and I know it'll never hurt me. And I never hurt inside myself, that doesn't happen in the water. Even when the boys circle my canoe in their speedboats, I don't get scared, I love it, it's like a contest. And I always win cause they can't tip me. See I'll take the canoe out with one of my friends like Bertha with the old lady frumpy name who can't even Swim! I never met a kid who couldn't swim but I took her anyway and she was safe with me. We crossed the Sound to City Island and back and the only time they tipped us was once when Sonny and about six of his friends swam out and attacked the boat

†
JMJ

and flipped it over cause I was laughing too much to concentrate on paddling faster. I love it that they try to tip me cause that lets me feel like one of the regular girls they pay attention to and that makes me feel kind of normal. And pretty. And I like that they can't beat me, I feel strong and I like feeling Strong.

†

JMJ

The Flesh

God doesn't want us paying attention to the body Dad says. It always gets you in trouble just like Adam and Eve eating the apple, cause it's <u>The Flesh</u> so it gets you to commit sins like Sex and Immodesty and Drinking Too Much. Sometimes it even makes you want to do things that are really Dirty like look at Condemned movies or pictures of naked ladies. But that wouldn't be a problem for girls, I never heard of girls looking at pictures of naked ladies and for sure they wouldn't be looking at pictures of naked men. Mom's really careful about all that seeing too much of the body stuff. So's Dad, he's the most careful when we're watching TV at night, all of us kids and Mom after the Rosary and home-work. Dad never watches TV, he just sits in his chair in his corner reading his prayer books. But if a couple on the screen starts kissing or hugging or anything he'll get up and stand in front of the TV and start winding the alarm clock like it's time to go to bed. He'll just stand there waiting for Mom to get up too and turn off the movie, like it's her job and then if she doesn't, he'll almost yell, What are you watching this Junk for? and turn it off himself. Mom I think gets a little mad at him cause she likes to watch movies with love in them where they kiss a lot. But Dad thinks it's a sin I guess or a Near Oc-casion like if we watch couples kissing, we'll want to be doing that too. And it must be a really bad thing cause Dad sure gets mad when he sees it. We never see him and Mom doing that and for sure you never see their bodies.

That's why you have to tell him what rating a movie has before you can go. A's okay and B's only for grown-ups and C's Condemned which means if you go even if you're a grown-up, you commit a Mortal. Those are the movies with all the Sex stuff in them. And you can't pretend you went by accident because all you have to do is read The Catholic News to see what the Legion of Decency says about the movie. Even if you don't get The Catholic News you can read the Legion of Decency list at the back of the Church when you go to Mass on Sunday. Of course nobody in our house ever goes to anything but an A except if someone like Sonny sneaks in without Dad or Mom knowing about it. But I don't think even Sonny would go to a C movie. And they have some really weird names on the C list, like one called The Moon Is Blue. And I know that all the movies that have that actress Bridget Bardot in them are Condemned. But I can't understand why she'd want to be in a movie that's Condemned, isn't she even ashamed?

And I wonder why God makes it that people have to have Sex to have kids. There's no way I can believe Mom and Dad did that except they had to, we're here aren't we? But I don't understand God's telling us to watch out for The Body and here He is making people do That. But it's none of my business anyway to be telling Him how to do His job, that for sure would be a Mortal of Pride. I'll bet He has really good reasons for making us have Sex. So even though I can't imagine ever wanting to do It I know God'll understand I'm accepting it like a Sacrifice and doing it because I Love Him and He wants me to. Probably He doesn't expect you to want to do It, it's a little suffering for the gift of having a baby because having a baby's such a Wonderful thing. Even though it makes me really Scared. But I figure I won't think about that til it's time. Anyway at least you only have to do it once to get Pregnant. Who'd want to do it more than that? Probably no one except the ones who go to Condemned movies, Perverts which I'm sure are only men cause women would never want to look at that stuff.

But sometimes I get real uncomfortable when I'm watching movies that have love and kissing. I guess Dad's right to be so careful cause I know that when I'm watching alot of kissing all of a sudden I'll start feeling all funny <u>down there</u> and it'll be almost Beating like it has a Heart or something then all of a sudden I'll have to pee. I hate it when that happens like all of a sudden you can <u>feel</u> it. Or you wash it in the tub and sometimes you do it for a little too long and a little too hard and it's nice for a second and then you get all scared that you committed a Mortal and that makes you feel all Dirty inside yourself. But that only happened once or twice. Or a few times. It hurts too much inside to know I'm Disgusting and about something so Bad, I can see why Dad's so scared about the Body.

An Immodesty Mortal

om's mostly the same about The Body as Dad. I mean even though she likes to watch loving and kissing she's really really careful about Modesty. I think Modesty's something for girls more than boys. Like Catherine and I always have to have our bathrobes on if we come out of our room. Sometimes though I think we should be able to come out in our nightgowns cause they're flannel so there's nothing in a million years that can show through them. But Mom says that with boys in the house we always have to wear robes. The boys can't come out of their rooms without pajamas but they never wear robes. That's what I mean about Modesty being more for girls. And of course Catherine and I are modest around each other too and we never let the other one see us undressing. We tell each other to turn around so we can't see. And we always wear lots of underwear. Even to bed. Some kids like at sleepovers and stuff'll laugh when they see my woolies cause they don't wear underpants to bed under their nightgown or their pajamas. I guess they don't have moms who're careful enough about Modesty.

One time though something happened about Modesty that really upset Mom. Mr. and Mrs. Schadel are our next door neighbors, he's a Police Detective who taught me to dive when I was four. And Jerry and I are the favorite neighbor kids of the Schadels so they always have us over for supper and for going out on their son Georgie's boat. Well one Sunday Georgie and his wife Edna and their kids were visiting and Edna invited me and Jerry to keep her and Joanne company while she fed the baby. There were lots of people and kids around and she needed someplace quiet to feed him so she was going out to the car. I was really excited to be invited cause I love babies and I have a million babysitting jobs so I was hoping Edna would let me help her feed the baby. And Jerry just likes being with us.

Edna sat in the back seat with the baby on her lap and Joanne next to her and she told Jerry and me to sit in the front. But then she did the most Awful thing, she opened the top buttons on her blouse and then this kind of a flap thing she had on her bra! I tried not to watch but my eyes kept wanting to look even though I was trying to not let them, I never saw one before except my own which're so small and Flat as a Board Sonny says and of course Mom never shows hers and here was Edna doing it in front of Joanne and even the new baby and what about me and Jerry? She acted like she was just giving the baby a bottle but I could see skin and there was even skinny blue lines showing through the skin and then she showed a Nipple, not exactly showed it she just let it come out on its own and she put the baby's mouth to it and the baby just started to suck it like it was a regular nipple on a bottle and Edna started to talk again like this was the kind of thing a kid sees every day and there's no big deal about it and you can't think of anything to say except things you can't say like How can you do that and isn't that a Sin and Immodest and what if Mom finds out? And does this mean I committed a Mortal? And what about Jerry, I'm supposed to be taking care of him and here I took him into this car where a lady that everyone thinks is so nice is opening her blouse in front of us and her own children too and putting her baby's mouth on it to suck as if it was perfectly normal and I was sick to my stomach and this time I was sure I would throw up.

Jerry I think just looked out the window and then put his head on my shoulder just like Joanne and pretended he was asleep. Of course when we got out of the car when Edna was finished feeding the baby, Jerry and me never talked about it again it was too embarrassing, what could we say? Edna's our favorite and we know a terrible secret, she's very immodest and that's for sure a Mortal. And Mom was really Mad. Not that I ran in the house and told her, I wouldn't do that but she saw us getting out of the car. She wanted to know what we were doing in Edna's car and said I had to tell her the truth so I did, I told her everything and she got really really Mad. But she didn't say anything to Edna, you can't really talk about those things but she said we couldn't go out in the boat the next day. I got a little mad at Edna then for doing something so bad that made Mom say we couldn't go out in the boat. Georgie always lets me and Jerry and Joanne sit all the way up on the top so the waves'll splash us as we fly along the Sound but now after the Immodesty Problem we're not allowed to be in the boat or anywhere with Edna. And Mom says I'm right that Edna did do something really Bad and even Disgusting.

One of the Seven Deadlies

ut the biggest and the worst problem with the Flesh was the Girlie Pictures, they for sure ruined things forever between Mom and Sonny after she found them under his bed. It's true. It's Terrible but it's true. And it seems pretty Disgusting to me all those pictures of naked ladies besides for sure being a sin, probably even a Mortal. It's the worst thing that ever happened in the Cusack house and probably to Jesus cause whatever we're doing down here we're doing to Him too. Mom said Sonny should be Ashamed of himself and how would he feel if Dad saw these and how could he ever serve at Mass and how could he do this with Girls in the House? Then I think she called him a Dirty Pig like Dr. Rossi called me.

I think I know why Mom's so worried about Dad finding out about the Girlie Pictures, his heart would be <u>broken</u> and none of us want to see that cause we love him so much. But we're kind of Scared of him too like if you commit really bad sins maybe he'll almost hate you. That's what would hurt Sonny most I think, Dad hating him so Mom's being nice not telling on him and not making Dad hear something so horrible about his own son that he for sure would never get over. And how could he even <u>look</u> at Sonny anymore? Even though Jesus forgave Mary Magdalene so it's Dad's job to for-

give Sonny but maybe its harder if it's your own kid committing Sex Mortals like Lust so if you aren't God and are just
a regular very holy person which Dad is you'd have a really
hard time forgiving that.

Mortals

The bad part about Mom not telling Dad about the Pictures is that if Mom couldn't tell him, you know for sure that what Sonny did is really really Bad, even worse than you thought. That makes me really Scared about Sonny going to Hell maybe and being a Pervert and a Sex Maniac. Then all of a sudden I'll be thinking about Dad and I'll be picturing his mouth getting fatter and fatter til all of a sudden it's Screaming You mean to tell me that you've been hiding pictures of Naked Women under your bed? Aren't you ashamed in front of Our Lord on the Cross? You think He doesn't see this? An Altar Boy? And his face'll be getting redder and redder and the veins'll be popping in his neck and he'll be yelling with his voice squeaking You'd better see Father Murphy and confess this before you Serve Mass again. I'm ashamed that a son of mine could have such Filth in his mind! You won't be going to Holy Name with me on Sunday Morning til I see you confess it and pray for Absolution and how could Sonny's chest not be burning inside at how He betrayed Jesus in such a awful way and inside of Sonny's mind he'll be hearing Dad Shouting that Sonny's a Sinner Disappointing Our Lord and some spit even flying out and the eyes wide open and not even blinking and you'll be getting Scareder and Scareder for him hoping he won't die before he can get to Confession

A Pervert

I hope Sonny remembers how happy God is to forgive things that Dad almost can't forgive or Mom. See the thing about God that's so great is He never says That's Your Last Chance. Even to Murderers and Perverts. All you have to do is go to Confession and He'll forgive you, just like that. He would've even forgiven <u>Lucifer</u>, Sister says but Lucifer wouldn't say he was sorry and do Penance so his soul stayed a mess. So Sonny probably even confessed the Girlie Pictures already, I for sure hope so. He's been real quiet since then and even though nobody ever said a word about it after it first happened, I think about it a lot. It's like your brother is this really creepy person and a Pervert and I'm kind of scared all the time now that he'll try to look when I'm taking off my woolies for bed so Mom says Dad has to make that his next project, putting a door between our rooms. And nobody talks to Sonny either, except maybe Catherine. Then one day when Dad took Mom out for her Sunday afternoon ride, Sonny just got up from watching TV and instead of going out to play Stickball he went in his room and all of a sudden he was dragging his mattress through the kitchen and down the cellar stairs. And he didn't come back up, he just stayed there. When we all went down there to have supper that night, I saw that he'd put it in a corner where he can be by himself. That's where he sleeps now and spends all his time just listening to the radio when he isn't out with his friends or drawing.

And nobody stopped him, for sure us kids couldn't but not Mom and Dad either. I don't even know if they <u>asked</u> him why he did it, maybe they did when I was in the bathroom or something. I know I'd feel really bad if I moved my bed down to the cellar and nobody asked me why, almost like they're even glad. And it's almost like Dad and Mom didn't even notice. I think Mom likes it better if he isn't so close to the family specially me and Catherine. Maybe she's afraid of him like you just never know what he'll do next so maybe it <u>is</u> better that he's out of the way. At least it's better for Jerry not having to sleep in the same room with him anymore and be scared every night that any minute he's going to get punched. But still I feel kind of sorry for Sonny always being on the outside and living all by himself in the cellar. Of course he comes upstairs when we're not eating down there and Mom still always makes sure to fix him his pancakes and bacon for breakfast.

Sonny and Mom

ut I still feel sorry for him. It's true, even though Sonny's really Mean and I mostly hate him, I still feel bad
for him when Mom's mean to him. And she's mean to
him a lot. Cause he's always doing things that make her mad.
Like The Girlie Pictures and Smoking. I can't figure out how
she found out about him Smoking cause she knew about it
even before I started Snitching. Then she started catching him
for Stealing, she says he's the only one who could be doing it
cause sometimes she's missing money from her pocketbook or
from her dresser and she knows that Sonny was the last one in
that room. She says Jerry and I could never do something like
that. Of course Sonny always <u>swears</u> he didn't take the money
but that doesn't matter, Mom never believes him. The other
thing he always gets in trouble for is not getting good marks in
school. Mom wants Sonny to care more about school and he
just doesn't. But even though she's always mad and blaming
him for stuff, he's mostly still nice to her and brings her pretty
presents for her birthday and Mother's Day. Like for Easter
cause he knows she likes flowers he walked back and forth
to the Boulevard which is about a million miles away to buy
her something pretty. I guess he figured if he walked he could
use his carfare money to get something extra special. And he
did, he came home with a rose bush that Mom planted in the

front yard, it's so beautiful that it blooms great big bright yellow roses. That's so great cause lots of times Mom goes out on Monday mornings and picks a bunch of them and lots of the cherry colored red ones from the huge vine that's climbing up the whole side of the house next to the stoop. I'm always so surprised seeing her cutting the roses not even scared to put her hands right into the bushes and thorns. Then she'll give us big huge bunches of roses to take to Sister in school. That makes me so happy cause it means Mom's in one of her good moods. Anyway, even after Mr. Shaw's men broke the cement in our yard and dug up lots of the ground around it and Sonny's rose bush got all broken and crumbly and dead looking, it bounced right back with millions of buds and real dark green branches and the next minute there it was with millions of fat and happy roses. Probably cause Sonny was nice enough to give it.

The Statues

hen something happened about The Body that started out great then turned real bad. But still it ended kind of good cause it helped me with the Girlie Pictures and Maybe Sonny's a Pervert Problem.

See even though school's out so you're supposed to be feeling all happy and free going swimming all the time and no stupid subjects, I can't stop thinking about Sonny. Even though it's summer you just can't be happy when you have problems like a brother who's maybe a pervert and who your mother maybe even hates. But lucky for me Betty O'Shea saved the day. See Betty who's Mr. O'Shea's daughter is the smartest lady in Edgewater and maybe even the whole Bronx. She still lives with her Mom and Dad like all ladies do if they're not married but soon she's going to move to California which is extremely far away. And she's a Lawyer, not like the other girls in Edgewater who go to secretarial school or to work and I know if no one comes before me I'll be the second cause I'm for sure going to College. And Betty's glamorous and nice too and she can drive a car. Anyway I'm very lucky cause Betty likes me. I don't know why but she asked Mom one day if she could take me to the Museum on Saturday and of course Mom said yes. I was really excited cause I've never been to the Metropolitan Museum of Art, I love that name, it sounds pretty and very Important. I don't think any other kid in Edgewater has ever been to the Metropolitan Museum of Art so for sure I'm pretty lucky.

I wore my Easter outfit, the blue dress with the white coat with the big sleeves and huge pleats in the back and of course my Mary Jane Heels. But not my hat cause hats make you look a little young and Betty wasn't wearing one and you don't need one anyway cause you're not going to Church. And Mom bought me Nylons. I felt pretty going out for the day with my friend Betty, we took the train downtown just like Mom and I do when we go shopping. Then all of a sudden we were in front of these huge columns and a million steps and a big door. Betty said we'd go first to the paintings then the Sculptures. I didn't tell her but I wasn't too sure what the Sculptures were. Of course the paintings were so great. I can't even imagine how artists paint all those ears and eyes and fingernails and hair and even rosebuds and leaves and birds and eggs and tulips and corn. It's pretty Amazing and such beautiful frames all gold and curlicues. But my feet were hurting from the strap on my Mary Jane's being too tight so after we saw all the paintings, we went to the restaurant and ate tuna fish sandwiches with extra mayonnaise and potato chips and of course Pepsi but I only had a few sips cause I was afraid I'd ruin the whole day by having to pee a million times. Then Betty said It's time for the Sculptures and of course as soon as I saw them I knew they were statues.

But that was the end of my really great day. The Sculptures turned everything Bad. The problem was that they were all naked. Big huge statues with no clothes. Of course I know that they wouldn't have <u>real</u> clothes on them but the artist didn't <u>sculpt</u> any clothes only naked bodies. And even couples kissing and holding each other. With no clothes on so you

could see Everything, Backsides and Belly Buttons and even
Privates! I was so ashamed seeing the bodies especially the
men's, even <u>that</u> was showing, except for a few that had a leaf
in front. That seems pretty dumb, a stupid leaf covering it, a
stupid little leaf for sure doesn't take care of the Immodesty
problem. I stayed very quiet thinking about what the artists
had done and wondering why they would all carve bodies
without clothes. And they were so Big, Big and White and
made out of Marble Betty said and I'm really ashamed to say
it but its true so I have to I was starting to think the statues
were kind of handsome all the muscles showing and all of a
sudden the burning was in my chest and under my cheeks
my eyes wanting to look even with me telling them No and
squeezing them shut and I couldn't imagine why in the world
Betty would take me here and Mom would say it's okay for
me to be in a place like this. And my eyes trying to open
and even almost wanting to look for a second at the Privates
which I never saw before and are so Ugly and Weird that I feel
sorry for men having to have something so Awful. Maybe that
means God doesn't like them as much as women or maybe
He decided that that would be their Cross. And does that
mean that Jesus had one and all of a sudden a picture was trying to flash inside my eyes and Oh, my God! For sure that's
a Mortal and the Burning in my chest was all the way up to
my throat but Betty was acting like nothing was wrong I was
so upset my belly was getting ready to throw up so I finally
asked her, Didn't the artists commit Mortals making all those
bodies without any clothes? And I don't know why but Betty
giggled. She said that the artists don't commit sins, they're
even allowed to do that <u>because</u> they're artists. It didn't really
make sense, but I said okay cause I wanted to believe her. So
maybe artists <u>do</u> have some special permission from God, I

don't understand God making a rule like that but I'm not supposed to understand I'm just supposed to accept whatever He decides. When I told Mom about Betty saying God let artists do things the rest of us can't, that really proved it, she said Betty's right and I guess she is cause Mom didn't get mad at her for showing me the statues.

And the really good thing that happened after the Museum is that I started to feel a little better about Sonny and the Girlie Pictures. Maybe God gave him permission too and maybe Sonny was thinking about painting naked bodies, and that's why he had the Girlie Pictures so maybe he <u>didn't</u> commit a Mortal and he won't be going to Hell if he doesn't confess it. Then Mom won't have to be so mad and maybe he never would've been a Disappointment to Dad. But I didn't say it to Mom, she always gets so mad when she thinks you're siding with the bad one and not her. So I just kept it inside myself but I feel really bad like I'll get sick and throw up not helping Sonny out by standing up for him.

Ashamed

It's not only Sonny that Mom thinks is bad, even Dad who us kids always thought was totally and completely Perfect has done some pretty bad things according to Mom. I don't know what she's mad at now but she's yelling again about Christmas Eve two years ago. See Dad was late coming home from The Shop where he and Chick and the two Charlies and Mrs. Merton, the Boss were all having a Christmas party and having a pretty great time with of course beer and I think maybe even Whiskey. I saw him walking from the bus stop, his head crunched down like Mr. Regan's always is and he looked very very sad and a little bit shy. He was walking kind of funny and almost tripping when he stepped off the sidewalk into the gutter so I pretended I didn't see him. Which was really mean me acting ashamed of Dad. Then I thought what if he's having a heart attack or something, but he was walking like Marie's Grandpa Gus does when he's Drunk. And when we got in the house, he was wobbling and weaving in the kitchen and Mom was yelling that he should be Ashamed it being Christmas and the kids all home waiting for him to get the tree and it was a Sin that we would see him like that so Dad hid in the bathroom. I could hear him getting sick and throwing up and I was getting really Scared but Mom kept saying he should be Ashamed and I thought I could hear him maybe even crying and I was really scared he might have committed a Mortal.

See Getting Drunk is a really Terrible thing in our house, nobody <u>ever</u> does that except maybe Aunt Rose and we're pretty ashamed of that. And it was even during Advent when Dad says we shouldn't be celebrating. Lucky for him Father Jordan always has Confession on Christmas Eve night and that for sure was a very important present for Dad, no way does he care about anything as much as Communion. So he must have confessed it, maybe after he Slept It Off cause it would Break his Heart, really completely <u>Smash It</u> if he couldn't receive Communion specially on Christmas.

Big Fat Liar

I was really getting ready to punch Sonny today. See one of the cool things about him is that all of a sudden he'll start talking to you and laughing even but not at you this time just being happy that you're his friend and he doesn't even hate you. Maybe he even likes you and doesn't think it's so bad having a sister like you, even as tall as you are. Well, today he was acting like that but all of a sudden after Mom started yelling at Dad about that Christmas Eve, he was saying So what if Dad was drunk. What's the big deal about being drunk? Dad told me he used to steal change too from the top of Uncle Mike's bureau when he was a kid in Ireland. When Mike came home he emptied his pockets on the bureau and sometimes, when he went in for supper, Dad would lift some change. Well I can tell you right now I had about a million feelings in that second, mostly it was great I don't even know why but it was mostly terrible too. I couldn't believe my ears and I was hating Sonny again for telling me about Dad doing something so bad as stealing. Even if it was his own brother who maybe would have given it to him any-way. Or maybe Uncle Mike was a Stingy Stingo and would never give you a penny even if you begged him. But it probably isn't even true, Sonny's just a Big Fat Liar.

†
JMJ

Rosary Society Ladies

etting Drunk isn't the only bad thing that Dad ever did
according to Mom. Like when us kids are driving her
crazy and Dad's reading his prayer books or saying the
Rosary or walking around Edgewater asking people to give to
the St. Frances Building Fund instead of checking our homework or helping her punish us, A man who'd pray less would
do you a better turn, she'll always say. Or Charity begins at
home when he wants to put a few more dollars in the Church
Envelope. And even though he never answers her back he
doesn't stop what he's doing either, he'll just go right back to
praying or collecting and she'll keep complaining. And they
have problems about ladies, mostly the Rosary Society which
is a club for the Moms who are married to the Holy Name
Dads. They mostly cook the bacon and make the pancakes at
the Communion Breakfasts and bake cakes for the cake sales
and maybe buy a new statue for the Church with the money
or give it away to feed the poor people. And the Rosary Ladies
play Bingo mostly.

Well, even though Mom's a Rosary Society Lady too and
for sure someone I think who'd love Bingo if she ever played,
Mom doesn't go to the meetings even though Dad wants her
to. She has no time for gossiping with a bunch of women
who don't bother to bid her the time of day she says, she

doesn't have time to be throwing her chest out with these ladies who're always looking for someone to tell them how great they are. She can never understand how Dad can be so smart and not see they're first on line to receive Communion then gossiping about everyone they saw at Mass. They're not even off the Church steps when they start, she'll say, A bunch of Hypocrites, that's what they are. She even makes fun of the way they say Dad's name like Hello Geeene. And even though Dad doesn't say anything, I think he wishes Mom would like them just a little. I think he'd maybe like to go to their houses on Friday nights for coffee and cake but Mom always says Why would I want to go there? She has nothing to say to them, she has enough to do in the house so they never go. It's like Mom doesn't like anyone Dad likes, like she's maybe jealous like you get when your boyfriend likes someone more than you. I always feel so bad when Mom calls Dad a Sap for liking the other Rosary Society Ladies. Like she called Catherine. I don't like anyone calling him a Sap. I almost hate it.

Family

The thing about Mom working is that for a few hours after school every day, she's not there. That might seem like no big deal but it is. Before she started working she hardly ever went out except to Hearn's Basement or that time she took care of Lilly. Now though we feel like grown ups having the house to ourselves, even if Sonny does beat up on me and Jerry when we come home. Catherine tries really hard to keep us in line getting us to start our homework and not mess the kitchen and to stop fighting and Sonny to not beat up on us, but none of us really listen to her. There's Bedlam as Mom calls it when she's not around, none of us do anything we're supposed to like homework or jobs til a few minutes before Mom comes home. We know what time Dad's picking her up and it takes exactly 25 minutes for them to get home after her train gets in so it's pretty easy to figure out our free time. Catherine and I also know just how much time it'll take to clean up the house and get dinner ready and the boys know how much time it takes to change their clothes and feed the dog. Catherine only starts with the I'm the Mother When Mother Is Out routine when one of the boys isn't moving fast enough and Mom's due home any minute. If things aren't done exactly as Mom wants when she gets home, someone'll get a beating. Mom always has The Belt handy.

She calls it Old Ned and she's pretty grouchy when she comes home from work and doesn't want any Back Talk from us kids.

Anyway, it's funny but it seems like we're all really glad to be together on those afternoons without Mom. I think we even like each other and that means Sonny liking me and Jerry. The first thing we do after Sonny's finished with his Throwing Us Down on the Bed Games that no matter what even Catherine can't get him to stop is to get the toaster going and the kettle, then we turn on the TV. We never change our uniforms til just before Mom's due in the door. It's fun sitting on the living room floor in your uniform drinking huge mugs of tea and eating Wonder Bread toast with lots of butter melted completely through so that the bread's all flat and soggy in the center and kind of shiny on top. If the butter isn't completely melted it's a failure. You have to throw it in the garbage and get rid of that before Mom gets home and yells because of the starving kids in China or maybe Africa. Anyway we have to have our toast towers maybe ten even fifteen slices and our tea ready by four o'clock when First Love, our favorite TV show comes on, it's the story of Miss Marlowe who's glamorous and sad. Her boyfriends are very handsome and strong and they like saving her whenever she has problems. And none of us even move from the TV except in an emergency to pee. But at 5 o'clock we all jump up cause that gives us just 25 minutes so we run around throwing things behind the couch, under the beds and in the bottom of closets and most days the house looks perfect when Mom walks in the door.

It's funny, these are the afternoons when any of us can come home late instead of heading straight home after school and none of us do. All four of us rush home every afternoon ever since Mom started working, it's like we love being together.

Carpenter's Dream

One thing that's bad about me not being a Nun is now for sure I'll have to have Sex cause if you're married you have to even if you don't want to. If you get married you're supposed to have babies, that's the reason you get married in the first place. I guess I can get used to it, I mean, Mom must have and Dad too. There's four of us so they must have done it at least four times. The stuff you do at the beginning of Sex like kissing and hugging I think would be even fun. The bad part is having to look at <u>that</u> and that he has to put it *in* you which isn't a nice thing to be talking about but it's true. And be Naked. Him too. But maybe not, maybe you just have to lift up your clothes and you can do that in the dark so he doesn't have to see you and you don't have to see him and he doesn't have to know your chest maybe is really small which if you were a Nun would be okay.

See when Sonny's mad, he'll point at my chest and say it's Flat as a Board and looks like Two Peas on an Ironing Board and I'll be pretty ashamed that he noticed and thinks it's a joke. He's my brother but he's a boy too so what he's saying maybe the other boys're saying too. Cause you're finished if you're a girl and have a small chest, the boys only like big ones but mine're taking forever to grow. Mom keeps telling me that hers took forever too and look how big they got. Still I'm scared that

I'll really be finished. On top of being Tall and a Snitcher and having such Big Feet, no boy'll ever like me. So I do a lot of worrying about my chest, it's almost like being a failure as a girl. But thanks to Mom, the chest problem's sort of solved cause she got me a padded bra. And even though my real size is a 32 AA, we got a 32 A. It makes a big difference. The quilted part fills you out Mom says. I love that bra and even though Mom says I don't need to wear it every day only when I need to fill something out, I want to wear it all the time.

Joanie

oday was a great day. Totally Completely Great. It was the first day I wore my new bra. It's Sunday and I didn't change my church clothes all day. I was wearing my navy taffeta skirt that puffs out over my crinolines like a dark upside-down tulip and my first nylon blouse. It's pink with rows of ruffles down the front and a little pointed collar that stands up around my neck and tiny round pearl buttons even on the sleeves. The thing about the blouse though is that you can see right through it. Because of the ruffles the front's no problem but in the back you can see everything and I wanted to wear my bra, everyone would be able to see through the blouse that I had one. And that'd be great but I was ashamed to have it show completely. It would probably be Immodest and maybe even a sin if a boy looked so I wore my undershirt over it. I was kind of embarrassed wearing such a grown up thing like a bra with such a kid thing as an undershirt but I didn't want to wait to wear it til Mom could get me a full slip or a camisole to go under it. I wanted to wear them right away, the bra and the blouse, so I did.

And after Sunday dinner I went for a walk. We always eat early on Sundays, like at 2 o'clock and most of the other kids don't eat til 3 so I knew no one would be out. I love to go walking when none of the other kids are out. No one's looking to see how Tall you are and there are no bunches of boys hiding in the alleyway ready to yell Stretch! or Jolly Green Giant! And today I for sure didn't feel like a Giant. I just felt like a girl all soft and pink in my see through nylon blouse and my new bra. You might even think I was Delirious about being Tall and I think I almost was. I could see myself in the window of Mr. Ferrick's car and I really looked Pretty, not just my face and my hair but my Figure too. Anyway I walked out Pennyfield Road towards Tommy Dunphy's house, he lives just past the Crazy Lady. Of course I didn't go <u>right</u> to his house, he would've known I like him. And it's not like there's anything else but weeds and Lots past his house. But lucky for me he lives right across from Mrs. Cahill's candy store so you can pretend you need something and just go in there and get an Almond Joy and then maybe he'll see you. And did I say I wasn't wearing a sweater so you could really see my blouse and even my bra?

Well the amazing thing is that even though I had my whole plan worked out even walking past the Crazy Lady's house, just as I got to the wire gate that separates Edgewater from Pennyfield I heard a soft whistle in back of me, the kind that starts out high and fast then gets slow and kind of wobbles in the middle before it goes down like a boy whistling at a girl cause she's looks pretty. I couldn't believe my ears, but maybe it wasn't for me cause no one <u>ever</u> Whistled at me before. Of course I didn't turn around, what could be worse than turning around and it not being for you!? I just kept walking. But then it happened again and he was saying, Looking pretty snazzy Joanie and I knew it was for me. And it was Tommy! I could have died. No one's ever been that Excited in their whole lives. So of course I turned around. I act like it was no big deal that I turned around but it really was. I was so excited and nervous and happy and afraid for a second I was going to pee but I didn't and I did turn around and he smiled and I smiled too and just waved and said Hi Tommy and that was that. I didn't wait around for him to start walking away. What could be more embarrassing than standing there thinking you're going to have a conversation or something and he says Well, see you and starts walking away like he wasn't thinking of talking at all? Well that didn't happen, I just kept walking like Tommy whistling at me was no big deal but it was it was the Happiest Day of my Life.

Only Couples

ven though it's true that Tommy whistled at me and wrote our names in a Heart, it still doesn't end my No Boyfriends Problems. I mean Tommy wouldn't ever tell me he liked me and ask me to Go Out, cause everyone would laugh at him and start teasing him. Who ever heard of a boy liking a girl who's taller than him? And even though that's all totally and completely true, Mom still keeps saying that the kids are all jealous of me and wish they were tall as me.

One thing happened last Saturday that proves that Mom's for sure wrong about the kids all wishing they could be me. It was the Worst day of my life worse even than peeing in my pants in school. I had started to hang around a little with the rocky kids like Valerie and Virginia who sort of have a Gang with boys and you have to be kind of rocky to be included. Usually that means if you're a girl you're pretty and the boys like you. So I was pretty delirious when all of a sudden one day Virginia told me that she asked Valerie if I could hang around with them and Valerie said okay. I couldn't believe it. I was so so happy. She didn't exactly say I could hang out with them as if I was a regular member but I could sometimes, if they invited me. That way they could see how I worked out and whether they could let me become a regular member of The Gang. Well I did that a few days after school.

Then came the day they were all planning to go to the Zoo, All Couples. Of course Valerie said I couldn't go if I wasn't in couples, but she said she was going to talk to Warren who's her boyfriend and the most important guy in the crowd to ask him what to do with me and maybe he'd decide that some boy would take me. The next thing I hear is that Warren told Jimmy Kelly to be couples with me and Jimmy said okay. Jimmy's kind of gawky looking and not a regular member of the crowd either, he was trying out too but I didn't care. Mom took me to Macys to buy a new blouse for it and even a new jacket, it was like Easter getting everything ready the night before. But then something awful happened. I was going down the stairs to the cellar to iron the creases out of my new blouse. I was singing and swinging my arms back and forth and the blouse was like a flag waving around me and all of a sudden I felt a ping on my finger the one right next to the thumb. I looked down and there was blood everywhere all over the blouse and my hand and the stairs even I ran upstairs to Mom and she said Into the bathroom! Get me a towel! Or a rag! Anything! Dad get the car! and she was pressing my knuckle real tight below where the bleeding was and then she tied the hand real tight with the rag so it hurt and covered the whole hand fingers and everything in a big towel that was already getting wet with blood Blood was everywhere all over the sink and the bath mat and even splashes on the wall and all over the front of Mom's housedress I was getting fuzzy in my head and thinking I was going to faint everything getting dark inside my brain and my hand pounding a lot and I knew right away it wasn't just an ordinary cut cause we weren't going to Dr. Green. What was really Awful was that when I got to the hospital and they put the stitches in my finger about 10 of them they said I had to stay there til the next day. I don't know why but the Doctor said something about it being a bad cut and alot of blood and the finger almost being ruined completely, something about not being able to move it anymore.

I started to cry that I couldn't go home with Mom and Dad and maybe the cut was so bad that I couldn't go to the Zoo tomorrow with Jimmy and Valerie and Warren and Virginia and that was the biggest reason for me crying and having to stay overnight for the first time in my whole life in the Hospital too! I didn't sleep most of the night, I kept praying that maybe by the next day the Doctor would say it was okay if I went to the Zoo. I'd be careful, I mean it was only walking looking at animals. And I didn't know what I'd do about the blouse but maybe Catherine would let me wear one of hers. But maybe the Doctor would say I couldn't go, then no way I'd ever have a chance to be part of The Gang again. This was my only chance so how could something this Terrible happen to me? But that's what God's for, for Emergencies like this so I prayed all night telling Him if He could just let me go to the Zoo with the kids I'd do whatever He wanted He could count on me. And I started praying to the Souls who I'd been helping get out of Purgatory. Maybe it would help them putting in a good word. I'd come home after the Zoo and go to bed and rest as much as God wanted and I wouldn't complain about kneeling for the Rosary Just Please Lord Please let me go.

But Mom and Dad weren't there at 6 o'clock like they promised. They didn't come til 10 and I just couldn't stop crying even though a nice girl in the next bed kept saying they would be here any minute. Then about 9 o'clock Valerie called, she said Mom told her that I couldn't go to the Zoo cause I cut my finger. Valerie said that was so Terrible she really felt Bad. I couldn't believe how Awful everything felt inside me all dark and sad like you woke up on Christmas and there were no presents or everyone forgot it was your birthday. Nothing as great as going to the Zoo with the rocky kids and having a boy who wanted to go with me had ever happened to me. Now because of my Stupid Finger, I couldn't go with Jimmy who I was starting to think was even a little bit cute. Then Valerie said, I blame Jimmy you know. Warren said that when he first told Jimmy he'd have to take you, Jimmy said, No Way! He didn't want to. But Warren told him he had to. If he wanted to be part of The Crowd and go to the Zoo, he had to go by the rules and the rules said Only Couples so he had to take you. But Jimmy was Mad. That's why I blame him for you hurting your finger cause he didn't really want to take you. Warren made him. It's his fault and it serves him right. Now he can't go either cause you can't go. That's what he gets for being so mean! It was hard not crying really loud cause my chest was rocking kind of back and forth and the cry was ready to burst out but I held my breath a lot and kept my mouth closed but she heard me anyway Are you crying? she asked but before I could answer she said I guess your finger really hurts a lot and even though I knew I was lying No way I'd let her know why I was crying so I lied and told her my finger was hurting too much and I couldn't talk anymore on the phone. God had decided not to answer my prayers, He even decided to let something extra bad happen. Not only that He didn't let me go to the Zoo but He let Valerie tell me about Jimmy hating me and not wanting to go with me and there are only two reasons I can think of that He would let all that happen. Maybe He needs me to do some extra suffering or maybe He decided I don't deserve it with all the bad thoughts I've been having not wanting to be a Nun, God sees that I'm not good enough or I don't pray hard enough. Mom and Dad finally came at 10 o'clock telling me that they were outside at 6 but no one would let them in til then.

†
JMJ

Mom was talking about making my favorite chocolate chip cake and Dad was calling me Pet and kissing my forehead and lacing my shoes and the doctor was looking at my finger saying Thank God You're a Lucky Girl You're finger's going to be fine but I just wanted to be alone so I could cry cause there was nothing else that I could do the tears just kept coming like there was an Ocean inside my eyes and my chest hurt and shook up and down a lot from the crying and not being able to breathe I don't know if wanting to die is the same as feeling like you don't want to live or don't think you <u>can</u> live but I know for sure I wanted to go away by myself some place very far away

Loser

nd Christian Fellowship didn't help. Christian Fellowship is a club Marie and Mary belong to at their church and they wanted me to join too but I can't cause I'm Catholic. I think it's even against my Religion to belong to a club in any other church. But they have meetings sometimes on Sundays and you can bring friends so they asked me to come. I'm surprised that Mom and Dad said I could but I guess it's okay as long as I don't join and only go once in a while. But then I found out that boys go too and that made me not want to go. And now they're all planning this dance for Friday night and Marie and Mary are all excited and want me to go too. If I wasn't So Tall, it would be okay but I am so it isn't. But they just went ahead and asked Mom if I can and she said Yes and that means I can't say No. And this isn't the only time that happened, Mom just won't ever let me stay home if there's a party or a dance I'm invited to. It's not that she says You have to like she's ordering me, it's just that she gets so excited like it's this really great thing and acts like that's how I feel too. I try to tell her I don't want to go because no one will dance with me but it doesn't help, she'll just be going on and on about how Of course you'll go and you'll have fun too some nice boy <u>will</u> dance with you. We'll go shopping Thursday night and get you something pretty. So we do. For the Christian Fellowship dance we bought a white fluffy blouse with long puffy sleeves and tight cuffs with tiny gold and pearl buttons and lots of ruffles down the front and a black skirt that's very soft and smooth and has a high waist and straps over my shoulders like suspenders. I love it and the blouse too.

But no matter how nice the clothes are they don't help, the boys ask all the other girls to dance and this time even Marie and Marie's kind of fat and not very pretty and she doesn't have new clothes. But this fruity kid with black shoes that have all those holes in the front and the extra piece of leather sewed on to the top like giant eyebrows asked her and she didn't care, at least it's a boy asking her to dance so who cares what he looks like but I just stood there feeling Taller and Taller as if I was growing every second and the almost normal way I felt when I put on the clothes in the store was gone and I was looking Clumsier and Clumsier and more and more Gawky every second and my head was almost reaching the ceiling I was so much bigger than anyone anywhere and praying for her to come back from her dance so I didn't have to stand there by myself anymore everyone looking and laughing at the Huge Beanstalk Girl in the corner.

And Mary's <u>always</u> dancing. It's hard sometimes to be friends with her cause she has nothing wrong with her, she's normal size and she's pretty and she isn't even fat. And the boys like her. I think even Sonny likes her, just as a regular girl you don't mind talking to, not like Marie or me who you don't want to have anything to do with if you're a boy. At least if Marie isn't dancing, you can stand there talking as if you're really interested in everything she says and you don't even care about some stupid old dance and you don't even want some boy to ask you you'd rather just keep on talking to your best girlfriend so it feels pretty awful when Marie gets asked to dance. Sometimes you'll be lucky and there'll be something posted on the bulletin board that you can walk over to and read like you really care about what it says and are really glad to have this chance to read it. But what you can never let anyone know is how bad you feel being left there by yourself and how your chest's Burning and the fire's almost in your belly and you have to go to the bathroom and the tears want to burst right out of your eyes but you have to act like you couldn't care less and you can't tell anyone not even Marie and for sure not Mary cause she'd never even know what that feels like she'd just be feeling sorry for you which is the worst thing ever. And the Burning doesn't stop when the dance is over there's still Mom.

When I get home, Mom's always waiting all excited and knitting some new sweater her fingers rushing round and round like they're running in place or nervous and it's perfectly normal that she's sitting up humming and sewing or knitting at 10:30 at night and Dad sound asleep on the Castro. And the light'll be on over her head making her look small and kind of pretty and maybe even shy but she'll be busy as if she doesn't even hear me come in then she'll look up like she's surprised and she hasn't really been waiting and I'm always so sorry to have to tell her ashamed like I am in the morning when she asks if I wet my bed and I have to say Yes and it hurts real bad inside my chest like something heavy like cement fell on it but I have to make myself say it No Mom Nobody danced with me.

Mom never says anything much after I tell her, just something like Well maybe next time or Oh they don't know anything, just a little something to make it sound like the whole night wasn't really a Huge Big Deal and a Complete Failure like I know it was. I'll bet she's getting pretty annoyed about all the failures, no matter how hard we try or how many new outfits we buy. Maybe she's starting to give up too on me <u>ever</u> having a boy like me cause last time I told her that no one danced with me, she said Don't worry you always have your books. And I'm even starting to feel a little mad at her for saying it, like books are as good as boys liking me and it's almost like she's making me ashamed of liking books like maybe I'm a Fruit or a Loser or something and I'm scared even Mom's giving up on me

Like a Girl Almost

ven after all the Failures Mom still never lets me be ashamed of being tall. She's always taking me out to buy me beautiful clothes whenever she thinks I'm feeling bad. And we can't even afford them, Dad's always working overtime or moonlighting and here's Mom spending all this money on expensive clothes for me. And even though I know Mom's doing it to make me feel normal I almost feel Weirder like a really junky present wrapped in sparkly paper. And I don't think it's fair either that the store makes a Huge Big Deal that you're Tall just like Footsaver does that you have Big Feet so they charge you a whole lot more money just for a few stupid inches. But Mom never complains about how much my clothes cost as long as I like them. And she's always saying I can wear Anything. Mostly I think she's just saying that cause she's my mother.

But every once in a while like maybe a year or a month even after one of those stupid dances, I'll almost forget about feeling Ashamed and looking like a Gawk and I'll be almost thinking maybe she's even right. I know she is about the black satin dress with the great big collar that's so full and graceful, it's almost like a cape that comes down almost to my elbows and then it comes in real close at the waist and then out again. And it has this really beautiful bright pink rose at the waist. I feel really Pretty in that dress and even a tiny bit feminine and feminine's always small and soft. And that's so great cause it's a feeling you never get to have cause you always have to wear dark color clothes even though your totally favorite color is pink. But you'd never in a million years think of wearing something so girlish as a pink dress, only small girls can wear pink dresses. It's true that you'll wear a pink blouse or sweater cause it's always with a black or navy skirt so it looks more tailored but never a whole complete dress or coat.

Except for one time when I did wear a pink dress cause Mom and the saleslady were really crazy about it and they kept begging me to try it on and they both said it looked great on me, and it's true a little bit of me thought so too even though most of me thought I looked really Dumb. But Mom liked it so much I thought maybe it was okay for us to get it. I loved the way the pink felt flowing around my legs. Like I was maybe Loretta Young! It's that thin almost see through material that nightgowns are made of and I was loving it touching my chest and my shoulders and how pretty my hand looked like my skin was almost pink and my nails too when I rested my hands on the dress. And it had a matching sweater that you could wear on your shoulders. Over your shoulders is a lot more glamorous. It's like the one Catherine lent me the day after I had my accident, it's the same pink color and I had the same Pretty Girl Feeling inside it.

But when Sonny saw me in the dress, he started pointing at my chest and he was laughing that loud stupid Veins Popping in His Neck Kind of Laugh and when he finally took time to breathe after all his dumb choking from howling laughing he yelled You look like an Overgrown Alice in Wonderland! And I could feel the red from the burning in my neck and my ears and it flew into my cheeks before I could stop it and I knew he could see the bright red color of my stupid skin like when I blush from someone saying a curse word or a dirty joke and I'm ashamed at hearing it and I can't believe I was so dumb thinking I could wear a small girl's frilly dress and I Hate that Sonny of all people saw me and is probably still Laughing and what I Hate Most is that he knows I want to look like a soft frilly girl when all I am is a Big Clumsy Oaf. I don't like Sonny knowing what I wish I looked like and I hate it that he won he saw my red face and he knew that he got me and he still knows, every time he looks at me he knows all over again and he's Glad I know for sure he's Glad and I think I might even Completely Hate him. Of course I took the dress right off and wouldn't wear it again no matter what Mom said and she sure was mad, mostly at Sonny but at me too for listening to him and for not wearing a perfectly good brand new dress that looked so nice on me she said but I just couldn't go around having the whole world laugh at me thinking I'm this Big Gawk trying to look like a girl. It took a really long time for the burning to stop this time almost as long as when I peed in school and Valerie said Jimmy hated me and every time I think of that dress the burning starts all over again

Everything's Too Small

For sure Catherine would never be caught wearing some stupid little girl's pink frilly dress, she only wears rocky Sheath or A-lines and always in dark colors and sweater sets and straight or poodle skirts. And white bucks or saddle shoes with knee socks. I kind of like Catherine's clothes even though they look kind of cheap and they're not 100% wool like Mom uses when she makes clothes for me cause Catherine thinks store bought clothes are better than homemade. Even I do a little, like when Mom buys cookies or cakes from the Krug's truck instead of always baking them herself. I mean Mom's stuff's great but it makes you feel kind of poor that you can't have store bought cakes and your Mom has to make everything herself even your clothes. Not all of them just some.

Anyway, sometimes Catherine wants to borrow something like my blue sweater set or maybe my black suspender skirt and I always say Yes, I figure you have to be generous. But Catherine isn't, even though she totally is with presents, she still never lets you borrow her clothes. I'll mess them up she says, or get them all wrinkled and smelly cause I'll never hang them up. But I don't hang them up cause there's never any room in our closet or when I do hang them they get completely smushed from being so close to about a million other things that we're always trying to find room for in our itsy bitsy closet. Which isn't even in our room, it's in the hall by the kitchen. Dad built it and that was great cause we sure needed one living in such a tiny house with practically no closets except the one he built by the living room. That's for him and Mom, it's the Linen Closet too and the Coat Closet. So everything including people gets smushed in our house cause of it being for tiny tiny people like <u>dwarfs</u> maybe but for sure not six Huge people with a million things to put away.

Only Water and No People

Everywhere around me all the time are walls and rooms and too many people. And there's always someone there in the same room with you folding the wash and doing homework and practicing piano and drums too and drawing and watching TV and cooking dinner and talking on the phone. Even after all the work Dad did on it, our house I mean, it still stays little. So besides going to the bathroom or taking a bath, you always have someone around. And even when you try to stay longer in the bathroom, there's always someone banging on the door saying you're taking too long. Lots of times they just barge right in unless you scream your head off that you're in there and Don't come in! And the houses outside are so close together that if Mr. Schadel moves his chair back from the table, we know that they finished their dinner and we can hear Mrs. Schadel scraping the dishes off before she washes them. I don't know what people hear coming from our house, besides all the Irish music, maybe Mom getting mad at us or us saying the Rosary at night which is kind of embarrassing even though it shouldn't be. So for sure you have to be careful what you say in your own house or your own room cause maybe the Schadels will hear you or the Bubels in back or even that old Busy Body Mrs. Hagess.

So if a person wants to do some thinking, they have to find

a place where they can be by themselves. I don't know if all the kids and grown ups feel like this too cause we don't talk about not being so crazy about your own house but how could they not be going crazy too every once in a while wishing for a place by themselves? That's why the beach when everyone leaves is so great. My favorite thing to do is to sit all the way out at the edge where all I see is Water and no people. Or I choose one of the jetties. They stretch all the way out into the water almost to where the boats are moored. It's a game I play every day trying to find the perfect spot where I can't see one living person in front of me or to the left or right when I turn my head. I'm surprised that I'm the only one to think of the beach but I must be cause most of the time nobody else shows up.

And Peace and Quiet aren't the only things I love about the Water, I love that it's huge and going on forever and taking me wherever I want to go. But sometimes I don't want to go anywhere, I just want to be right there sitting at the edge of the bulkhead or jetty with the water stretching out all around me like this big beautiful table all glistening and ready for me to spread out all my thoughts. And it's so great having all that space around me with lots of room to stretch my arms and legs and still they won't touch anything. Not one thing. And with all that room, I even feel kind of small. It's true. I mean my body isn't too big for the space like it is in the desks in school which're for midgets not real kids and for sure not Too Tall ones. And the streets in Edgewater where only one car can go through at a time and a million other things that make my body seem like it doesn't fit. So sitting here with all this water stretching out around me makes me feel normal size and I know I keep saying it but I can't help it <u>Cross My Heart</u> sometimes even small. Almost like a Girl and never in a million years could I ever get tired of that. So I always thank God for being so kind that He gave me the Water. And that isn't even something I prayed for, I never even knew I needed it. But He did, He's always there just watching out for me, deciding what I need then giving it when it's time.

†
JMJ

Being Awful

B
ut I can't stay at the Beach forever. God needs me to
go back home and be Joan Cusack again, living in a
tiny tiny house with about a million other Problems
I'm always worrying about. And how I made them Worse.
Especially the Catherine and Mom Maybe Hating Her One
which is maybe the hardest secret to tell.

Anyway, the first time was about Catherine being nice.
See Catherine's so nice she sent a postcard to Mr. Regan that
time we went on vacation to Old Orchard Beach way up in
Maine. He's the real old man up the block who smells from
pipe and whose wife died which is really too bad. But when
Mr. Regan told Dad about it and Dad told Mom, she started
Laughing. That made me feel pretty bad for Catherine cause
I hate it when someone laughs at me. But she's the Mother
and it's true Catherine was a little bit Silly so she should
be Embarrassed cause she did something that's pretty weird
sending Mr. Regan a postcard and all of a sudden we were all
Laughing at her for being so friendly and that gave me a really bad feeling inside myself like in a second I'd Throw Up.
It's too bad but when Mom starts to laugh about something,
we all do too cause you know you have to feel the same way
she does. Or at least act that way. But maybe you _do_ have the
same feelings someplace deep inside yourself. And I'm really

Ashamed to say it but it feels even a little fun to be a tiny bit mean. Or if it really bothers you that what she's doing isn't fair you can just not say anything or go in your room and pretend you didn't hear what's going on. That way you can not let her know you don't agree with her and not let the kid who's getting in trouble or being joked about think you're siding with Mom.

The worst thing that happened though was about my birthday which was a pretty long time ago but I was too ashamed to talk about it. See every year when it's their birthday, Catherine and her friends get each other corsages, Special Corsages, like for 16 there's sugar cubes and for 12 tootsie rolls and 15 maybe bubble gum. And 14 is <u>dog biscuits</u>! That seems like a pretty crazy thing to make a corsage out of but that's the rules. You can tell how old a girl is by her corsage. Sometimes you get lots of them cause all your friends buy them for you, that's always so much fun walking around school like you're really really popular with a bunch of different corsages pinned to the front of your uniform. I totally love them and couldn't wait to get my first one. They're the best part of your birthday but they don't start til you're twelve and I couldn't wait, I knew I could count on Catherine to get me one, even if my friends forgot.

Well Catherine and all of her friends had started going to football games a lot and all the girls who had boyfriends were wearing Football Flowers, Gigantic Bright Yellow Mums with about a million happy petals. Now the thing is my birthday comes at the same time as they do, in October when it's Fall and all the leaves are turning colors specially yellow and everyone's starting to go to football games so Catherine decided to get me a Football Flower instead of tootsie rolls. I can see how she could think I'd be dying to have a Football Flower like the older girls get from their boyfriends but I didn't really want to be like the older girls, I wanted to be like the other girls in my school who get tootsie rolls when they're 12. So I hope I didn't act too disappointed when Catherine gave me the corsage but it's true I was a little bit embarrassed about wearing a Football Flower when everyone was expecting me to come in with tootsie rolls.

I didn't know what to do except I knew I'd have to wear it and I did talk a little to Mom about feeling bad and embarrassed. I just wanted to talk to her about the problem, just the two of us I mean it's not like telling your friends which you would never do but telling your Mom you figured was okay. But then Mom went to Catherine and yelled at her for giving me the Football Flower instead of Tootsie Rolls. She made it sound like Catherine did a mean thing and she wanted to be Mean and it meant she Hates me. <u>How could you do that to your sister?!</u> she yelled as if Catherine had called me a mean name or something. Then she said, still yelling I was going to be Embarrassed in front of my friends if I had to go to school wearing that corsage and the burning in my chest was back and in my belly and I was saying No Mom it's okay it's a nice corsage Catherine didn't mean it I'm sorry Catherine but Catherine was looking all confused and hurt and her eyes were squinting and her face getting really red like mine does and I think maybe she was crying and after that I can't even remember what I saw or what I did or what happened to the corsage. It's like nothing else happened after Mom yelled at her and Catherine looked at her and me with the hurt That's Why I Know I'm Adopted look on her face then everything was dark and black inside my head and that was the only picture left Catherine hurt and Mom yelling at her for hurting me by buying me the wrong corsage and everything black and the red hot fire inside my chest down into my belly it was my fault I was Selfish not being grateful to Catherine and making Mom yell at her. Even though I didn't really <u>make</u> Mom yell at her, I should never have told her how I felt about the flower, you should <u>never</u> tell <u>anyone</u> how you feel.

Kind of Normal

I still feel like a Traitor to Catherine. I hope she doesn't completely Hate me like I hate myself everytime I think of the corsage. One thing's for sure though, ever since then I make sure I <u>never</u> tell Mom stuff. It's even kind of normal I think to have secrets from your Mom. Like who smokes and who you like or who you think is cute. I mean you'd never tell her who Virginia picked for best friend and that it wasn't you, but still she picked you maybe to be second. And Virginia's one of the rocky kids so it's even great to be picked as second or third or even fourth. But you must be getting a little bit cool cause they're even calling you up saying come down to the candy store to hang out. And for sure you do, even if you feel Stupid and Gawky not knowing <u>how</u> to hang out like talking to everyone, the boys too and laughing like you're not even so Nervous you have to pee. So you watch Virginia and Valerie and do what they do.

But Mom doesn't understand rocky and not rocky cause she thinks I'm Better than them and they don't even Deserve to hang out with me! So I have to keep any problems a secret cause once Mom hates someone, she'll never stop. She might even not let me hang around with Marie anymore if she found out about her Mom being mean sometimes. And for sure she'd hate the Mom for saying my coat doesn't go with my face or my feet are really big or I have a huge amount of freckles. Even after I wasn't mad at her anymore, Mom would still be. Look at how mad she got at Catherine who's her own Daughter when Catherine made the mistake with the birth-day corsage. At least I never told her about Sonny playing his Throwing You Down on the Bed Games. She would have Hated him even more.

Disappointing Dad

It's funny, being good isn't the same to Mom and Dad. Like Dad doesn't worry about Friends or if we hang around with the Wrong Crowd and if we do something Behind His Back, Dad won't blame it on our friends like Mom does, he'll blame it on us. Dad only worries about sins and praying enough and keeping all the Commandments and always thinking about Heaven and Hell. And not boyfriends and kissing and what you look like and mirrors and thinking you could maybe be a Model. The body's a Temple of the Holy Ghost, Dad says and it's a Sacrilege to use it for anything else like the Evil Ways of This World. So for sure Dad doesn't worry about clothes and me looking great and being too tall cause that's just Vanity, caring too much about how you look.

So Mom must be committing sins against Vanity too, not for herself but for me. See Mom doesn't care much about holy, not that she doesn't want you to be but she doesn't worry about it. And she's not thinking about where you go after you die. She's just worried about you being good this very minute and tomorrow and last week. So it's two kinds of good, inside and outside now and forever and Mom liking the Outside best and the life we have while we're living now and Dad liking the Inside and the life waiting for us after we die. The Afterlife's the only Real Life he says.

And sad to say, I think Dad'll think it's his fault if we don't get into Heaven. Like he was a Bad Father not teaching us enough like Mom feels that I'm not popular or if we get sick. Or I don't like myself so it's her fault, she didn't try hard enough. But I don't think it's Mom's fault if I'm Too Tall and the kids tease me. And she can't make it go away, no matter how she tries, God gave it to me so I have to have it. And it's not Dad's fault that I don't want to be a Nun and I'm not sad at all when I'm sick and don't have to go to Mass or say the Rosary and lots of times I totally forget about the Souls and I love clothes and looking in the mirror or that I might really want to start kissing boys. Dad tried real hard to get me to be the girl that Jesus wants, who for sure should be praying for a Religious Vocation and shouldn't be liking boys and kissing so much. And even though I still go to Mass with him during Advent and Lent, I don't feel so close to him anymore cause I don't think he'd be too crazy about me if he could read my mind and find out that I was caring about all this Flesh stuff. So it's better to not let him and Mom know what I'm thinking about and maybe wanting. It would really hurt them alot to think they failed. Mom and Dad both tried to fix the feelings I have inside myself, it just didn't work.

Happy

very Friday night all the older kids, like Catherine and Kitty and Tommy Schilling and Bob Annesi and the rest of their Crowd go down to Big Oak to Make Out. Big Oak's our beach and it's named after our favorite tree that's standing right there on the bulkhead shading everything that needs shading. Anyway Friday's Make Out doesn't even have to be boyfriends and girlfriends, maybe you want to try someone out to see if you can like them. So it's kind of good that there are no rules, except I don't think they should be Making Out in the first place, but it isn't my business cause I'm not part of their Crowd and I wouldn't be doing it anyway. Well, last Friday Catherine and Kitty went to the movies instead of going to Make Out, maybe they were getting bored with it and wanted to do something else for a change. That night I was coming home from Braren's around 7 o'clock and when I got to the top of the hill, I met Lloyd who said Hi. That was quite a surprise cause he never even spoke to me before. Then the next thing he said was Where's your sister? and I said, At the movies. Then he said What about Peluso? and I said Her too. I knew he wanted to know who he was going to be Making Out with that night and from the way the questions went Catherine came first and then Kitty. Anyway the next thing he said was the Killer <u>What are you doing later?</u> I could have Died He meant he wanted me to come down to the beach later and Make Out with him I couldn't believe my ears Lloyd Dean wanted to Make Out with me! And he's the second greatest swimmer in Edgewater and the second cutest, the first is Cliff his brother and all the older rocky girls are totally crazy about the Dean Brothers and dying for a ride in their boat Peg of My Heart. And Lloyd asked <u>me</u> to Make Out!!

But I said I'm busy. Just like that, I said No to Making Out with Lloyd Dean! Even though it's true that I don't know how cause I never did it before and that could be pretty Embarrassing specially in front of a guy as important as Lloyd, that's not the reason. And it's not even because Making Out I'm pretty sure is a sin, specially if you're kissing and hugging for a few hours. It's too bad but I wasn't even thinking about God. I said I'm busy because even though I was thrilled that he would even <u>think of</u> Making Out with me, I didn't want him thinking I'm Hard Up. That's like saying I know you can't find anyone else and the only reason in a million years that you're asking me is because you're Desperate but that's okay because I'll never get anyone else anyway. And Hard Up's not what I'm ever going to be. No way Lloyd Dean'll think Joan Cusack will Make Out with you even though you never even spoke to her and wouldn't be caught dead with her if anyone else was around. It's like I was saying about Joyce. You always have to act like you deserve to be treated like a normal person, not like someone who's thrilled when some guy talks to you and asks you to Make Out just cause no one did before and he's cute and all the girls like him. I don't think I'd <u>want</u> to be Making Out with someone just to Make Out. And I don't think I'd want to kiss anyone for hours unless he <u>wants</u> to kiss me Joan Cusack.

I felt real strong and proud of myself and I walked the rest of the way home with my back real straight and my legs and feet kind of bouncy and my arms swinging along beside me like in a parade. And inside myself I was Happy and I remember feeling Pretty.

My Bathing Suit

The best part about the beach and God taking care of me is the biggest secret I've ever had. The biggest happy one. The Corsage one is the most ashamed. And only Jesus knows and Blessed Mother of course. And it happened last week when Mom bought me the most beautiful bathing suit you ever saw. So smooth, like my black satin dress. We were all crazy about it, me and Mom and the saleslady even and I was turning around and walking real slow real graceful like I always do for Mom and the salesladies and she was saying how Beautiful I was she'd give anything to be that Tall, I could be a Model. And it, the suit I mean, comes straight across the top with wide straps that you don't even have to tie if you don't want to if you want to get a really good even Burn or maybe even if you want to be a little bit Sexy. That's how I wear the suit. Except for swimming which to tell the truth, I don't do in this suit. Mostly I just keep it for my evening walks to the beach, so for Show. For regular swimming I just wear last year's suit, the grey and white two piece which is very cute but like a kid's suit. And the white one has a padded bra in it too so it doesn't matter that I don't fill out the top. And a huge red poppy that kind of springs across the suit like it just grew there. From the bottom of the stem on the bottom on my left side, it reaches all the way up and across to the tips of the petals across my right breast. It's kind of Embarrassing to say that cause it sounds Immodest but that's where it goes. It's the Most Beautiful Bathing Suit I ever saw.

It's true, I definitely have the nicest suit in Edgewater. And it cost 22 dollars! I feel kind of guilty that it was so expensive but the thing about it that I can't believe is that I think I might even look great in it and a little sexy and even glad to be Tall. I like it that my legs are so long and my waist so small, my chest feeling it too that I might even be Beautiful. I like when I catch myself in the mirror or sneak a peek at myself in the window. The first day I wore it, I took a walk along the bulkhead to the other end at Sandy Pier. I didn't want to go home so fast and take it off. I wanted to walk longer in it, maybe even forever. Like a Model walking along and the bulkhead's a Runway in a Fashion Show and I'm believing them, Mom and the salesladies at Macys and I'm just walking along looking Lovely not even noticing that eyes are following me.

Some Kind of Hope

hen I noticed that Ozzie was in his yard fixing his out-board and he was looking at me for a long time. And it's not that Ozzie's handsome cause he isn't. He's al-ways walking around in those Farmer Browns that Dad only wears on the job. Ozzie's a little bit of a joke too to most of the kids cause he's a man who wants to hang out with kids, Sonny's friends mostly. But the thing is, Ozzie never looks at anybody, he just keeps his head down all the time and works on his outboard and paints his boat. But this day he was look-ing at me and he even smiled a little. I liked it that he looked at me like he liked it too. It's kind of Embarrassing to say that but it's true. Of course all of this took only a very little time and for sure not as long as it's taking for me to tell it cause I kept on walking like nothing really happened and Ozzie went right back to fixing his outboard. And it's not like Ozzie was asking me to Make Out because of course he wasn't but it was nice feeling like you're Pretty and somebody besides your Mom thinks so too. Even though he's a man who I think might really want to be a boy. Well of course since then I walk along the bulkhead past Ozzie's house every night and what's really amazing is that every night some other man is out in his yard reading the paper or maybe fixing the fence or watering the grass. They're all there and I know it sounds Conceited but I know they're waiting for me. Their eyes'll look out from behind their newspaper maybe or up from the watering and they'll smile for a second and then go back to reading their paper or hosing the stoop and they'll look down almost like they're shy. I can't believe it but it's true, completely Grown Up Men looking at <u>me</u>. And I love it that their eyes don't want to stop looking at me.

My Kid Cross

So maybe if I can just get through the girl part I can get to be a lady and things'll be different. Maybe being a 6 foot tall lady's going to be even great. Even now I'm kind of happy sitting in my corner by the water with my legs crossed like the bathing beauties do just in case one of the men walks by on their way home from work or Lloyd or Cliff come in from the boat and I'm thinking that maybe God's even planning on making me happy when I'm a Grown Up. And the Tallness is only my Kid Cross. So I just have to suffer a little bit longer. Like Purgatory maybe, then Heaven.

†
JMJ

Acknowledgments

I t takes many people to make a book—readers, editors, copy editors, visual artists, and designers, not to mention family and spouses who graciously, or at times reluctantly, move over while this new love takes over his/her spouse and home. So, too, with *Confessions*.

Thanks first (as always) to my beloved Alan, who makes our abundant life possible and beside whom I grow out of the ground; to David, our son, my creative inspiration and most insightful reader; and his wife, my Marlene, who oozes life and laughter and just makes me giggle

Thanks to my editors, whom I credit with teaching me to write prose—Molly Peacock, my trusted mentor across all stages and genres of my writing; Mickey Appleman from whom I learned the invaluable contribution of a good editor; Baron Wormser who believed in me and *Confessions* from its inception; and Florenz Eisman who treated me with the same dignity and professionalism as she does all CKP writers

To my generous and trusted readers—many who have read and reread *Confessions*—particularly Carol Snyder and Teresa Carson, both of whom read the book in all of its many versions and whose knowledge of me and good writing helped

†
JMJ

strengthen the book; Catherine Breitfeller, my sister and one of the stars of this story whose sharp recall added a few vital details to my repertoire; Charlene Kutis, my daughter-in-law's mom and my newest friend, another girl of the 1950s who shared complete devotion to her father

To Carlos Andrade, whose art speaks from the heart of me

To CavanKerry book designer Greg Smith, a brilliant designer and lover of all literary art

To Bob Weibezahl for his generous and insightful press release

To Dawn Potter, who, despite impeccable copy-editing skills, had the wisdom to guide but not intrude on my rather idiosyncratic grammar and diction

To my loyal and loving assistant, Donna Rutkowski, whose efforts and spirit have made my busy life possible and who has served as keeper and shepherd of *Confessions* in all its many versions and travels

To Michelle Blake and Roland Merullo for their thoughtful readings of and comments on *Confessions*

To the following journals in which sections of *Confessions* first appeared:

Indiana Review: "Beanstalk"

Southern Humanities Review: "The Flesh"

Other Books by Joan Cusack Handler

CavanKerry's Mission

CavanKerry Press is a not-for-profit literary press dedicated to art and community. From its inception in 2000, its vision has been to present, through poetry and prose, *Lives Brought to Life* and to create programs that bring CavanKerry books and writers to diverse audiences.